THREE PLAYS

THREE PLAYS

DIVIDING THE ESTATE,
THE TRIP TO BOUNTIFUL, AND
THE YOUNG MAN FROM ATLANTA

Horton Foote

With a foreword by John Guare

NORTHWESTERN UNIVERSITY PRESS
EVANSTON, ILLINOIS

Northwestern University Press
www.nupress.northwestern.edu

Printed in the United States of America

10   9   8   7   6   5   4   3   2   1

Library of Congress Cataloging-in-Publication Data

Foote, Horton.
    [Plays. Selections]
    Three plays : Dividing the estate, The trip to Bountiful, and The young man from Atlanta / Horton Foote ; with a foreword by John Guare.
        p. cm.
    ISBN 978-0-8101-2536-0 (pbk. : alk. paper)
    1. Texas—Drama. I. Guare, John. II. Foote, Horton. Young man from Atlanta. V. Title.
    PR6056.O85A6 2009
    812.54—dc22

                                                    2008039044

CONTENTS

FOREWORD

John Guare

Think of the plays that Tennessee Williams, William Inge, and Arthur Miller wrote in the 1950s. Spot quiz: an aging hustler returns home with a fading movie star and is castrated by the father of the girl he infected (you got it—*Sweet Bird of Youth*); a cowboy kidnaps a saloon singer and then gets trapped with her in a roadside diner during a snowstorm (of course! *Bus Stop*); a witchcraft panic ensues in eighteenth-century Salem (too easy—*The Crucible*).

The point is I can't imagine any of these events in a Horton Foote play. In the three plays in this volume: A family must face life under reduced financial circumstances. An old lady wants to get back to the home where she was happy. A couple contends with the offstage appearance of a young man from Atlanta who might have been involved with their late son. These are not extravagant Jacobean plots. Like most of Horton's plays, they are set in Texas, in and around a small town outside Houston, during the twentieth century.

But isn't great American literature all about the journey? Huck Finn and Jim on the Mississippi; Humbert Humbert driving across America with his Lolita; Sal Paradise and Dean Moriarty in Jack Kerouac's *On the Road*? Horton belies that. In *Dividing the Estate,* a character says, "There are fools that drive in every day to Houston to go to work. I say you wouldn't catch me driving sixty miles no place just to work." In *The Trip to Bountiful,* Carrie Watts's epic journey to the place where she once had been happy is only a bus ride away. In *The Young Man from Atlanta,* the son does leave Houston and travels seven hundred miles to Atlanta for a new life that will end in his mysterious death. But his parents make contact with another young man from Houston who had lived in the same Atlanta boarding house and who brings back news of their son. In anyone else's hands this could be the most blatant unlikely coincidence, but in Horton's world it's a basic fact of life. We can never escape anyone. We can never get away. In the early plays, this connection can be a blessing. In the later plays, it can be a nightmare.

I can pinpoint the date that I learned the name Horton Foote. The Dramatist Play Service acting edition tells me it was April 5, 1953. That was the night I watched *A Young Lady of Property* on Philco Playhouse. For the first time ever, I burst into tears in my home for nondomestic reasons. The fifteen-year-old girl in the play (my age exactly!) wants to get to Hollywood to pursue her dream of being a movie star (yes—that's me!), but gives that up when she must fight to keep her home (I'd do that, too).

Who wrote this? Who knows me this well?

The young actress who played Wilma was Kim Stanley. But who wrote those words? I knew about playwrights—Tennessee Williams, whom I read about in *Life* magazine, and of course Arthur Miller, who was married to Marilyn Monroe.

This playwright was Horton Foote.

I kept on the lookout for him.

It wouldn't be hard. In checking Horton Foote's TV career, I was astonished to learn that in the seven-month period from May to December 1953 Horton saw the following plays produced on prime-time TV: *The Traveling Lady, The Trip to Bountiful, A Young Lady of Property, The Oil Well, The Rocking Chair, Expectant Relations, The Tears of My Sister, John Turner Davis, The Old Beginning,* and *The Midnight Caller.*

Could I have seen all of them? It's possible. I loved television. I hated to go out of the house unless it was to a movie or a play. My parents would say, "You have to go out of the house sometime." "Why? Everything's here. Besides, I'm going to be a playwright." (I already had written three plays when I was eleven, and the local paper did a story on the eleven-year-old playwright.) Horton Foote made playwriting so easy. He wrote about people like the people I knew, even if they were from Texas, which allowed them to speak in fabulous accents, and he just set them talking. I loved the cozy size of Horton's world. I could manage a world that size. Yes, Horton's plays were the kind of plays I wanted to write. (I called him Horton; hadn't I met him in my living room?)

Time goes on. Love dies.

In January 1956, at age seventeen, I saw Tyrone Guthrie's production of Marlowe's *Tamburlaine the Great,* which came to Broadway for a very short run. I gasped at the sight of Tamburlaine unfurling an enormous map of the world across the stage of the Winter Garden Theatre, striding across it, claiming it all—

> *Forsake thy king, and do but join with me,*
> *And we will triumph over all the world:*
> *I hold the Fates bound fast in iron chains,*
> *And with my hand turn Fortune's wheel about;*
> *And sooner shall the sun fall from his sphere*
> *Than Tamburlaine be slain or overcome.*

Wait! That's the kind of play I wanted to write. Get me out of my living room. Let me stride across the world!

Forget Horton Foote! The size of Horton's world was only as big as our twelve-inch black-and-white television set. It was easy to consign him to the dustbin of a simpler time.

In 1957, when I was nineteen and a sophomore in college in Washington, D.C., I saw, in its pre-Broadway tryout, Jean Anouilh's *Time Remembered,* with Richard Burton and Helen Hayes. It was the most glamorous play I had ever seen, set in a château—a romantic love story of death and rebirth. A full orchestra in the pit played a score written by Vernon Duke. I went to every performance of it. It was French. That was the life I wanted—the theater I wanted.

Then I saw Peter Brook's 1958 production of Dürrenmatt's *The Visit,* starring Alfred Lunt and Lynn Fontanne. Imagine: The richest woman in the world returns to her poverty-stricken village. She'll give them a fortune. All she wants in exchange is the life of the beloved mayor of the village who'd been her lover when she was a girl and who had abandoned her. I had to learn to create a world like that.

But how? It was all so European.

The '60s came. My new masters were Albee and Pinter. My peers were Arthur Kopit, Jean-Claude van Itallie, Sam Shepard, María Irene Fornés, Rosalyn Drexler, Arnold Weinstein—American playwrights, some of whom I actually knew, all occupied in the business of carving out, creating a new American sensibility.

What happened to Horton Foote? I imagined that his work—like Paddy Chayefsky's (*Marty*), JP Miller's (*Days of Wine and Roses*), or Robert Anderson's (*Tea and Sympathy*)—forever belonged to the '50s. Small, naturalistic, the size of a TV screen.

In the '90s, I was in Chicago doing a new play, which began on an ice floe in Alaska and wound up in the Everglades with singing mermaids. Red Grooms had created sensational scenery. It wasn't working. How much of the fault was mine?

I took a long, raw walk through unfamiliar Chicago streets to clear my head. I wandered into a secondhand bookstore, checked the theater books. Nothing of mine. I saw a collection of Horton Foote one-acts, which included *A Young Lady of Property*. Should I look at it? I expected the shock akin to betrayal that you feel when you revisit a book or a play you had loved years before only to find the words you had once loved now strewn lifelessly on the page like sand. I had already outgrown Anouilh. It had happened with Bellow's *Henderson the Rain King*. Why not open *A Young Lady of Property* and look in on my fifteen-year-old self?

> WILMA: Maybe I won't go to Hollywood after all . . . Maybe I
> shouldn't. That just comes to me now. You know sometimes
> my old house looks so lonesome it tears at my heart. I used to
> think it looked lonesome just whenever it had no tenants, but
> now it comes to me it has looked lonesome ever since Mama
> died and we moved away, and it will look lonesome until some
> of us move back here. Of course, Mama can't, and Daddy
> won't. So it's up to me.

What shocked me was that the play had exactly the same effect on me in that Chicago bookstore as it had in our living room forty years before. If I did not burst into tears, I still saw exactly what had made me love this play and this writer. The young girl yearning to escape her life and find glory in Hollywood. Wait—had Horton dropped the seed for my play *House of Blue Leaves* into my unconscious that night in 1953?

I bought the book of seventeen one-act plays and read them.

Naturalistic? Hardly. The dialogue was boiled down to its essence, as packed and resonant as any in American drama. The plays were brutally nonsentimental.

There on the same shelf were the nine related plays of Horton's *Orphans' Home Cycle*. Why had I never heard of these plays? Am I crazy or are these nine plays one of the unheralded masterpieces of the American theater? Eugene O'Neill had a dream of writing a cycle of eleven plays of American life, but only the third play, *A Touch of the Poet*, was completed. It, and an almost finished draft of the fourth, *More Stately Mansions*, are all that survive. O'Neill called his family cycle *A Tale of Possessors Self-Dispossessed*. That could be the name for Horton's secure achievement.

I wish I could say that rediscovering Horton Foote in that used bookstore had solved my play's problems. No. My play got dreadful reviews, not only bankrupting but closing the Chicago theater that produced it. But what was my rekindled obsession with Horton's work telling me? When we hate something, we want it out of us, we want to forget it, and we express that contempt in no-nonsense excremental terms. But when we love something, what is that telling us? Was that kind of love saying *Make me part of you*? What could I learn from Horton?

I read *The Trip To Bountiful, The Habitation of Dragons*. I was astounded to find *The Chase*, the source for that rotten Marlon Brando movie, to be as passionate, simple, and elegant as the screenplay (by no less a light than Lillian Hellman) was bloated.

What is Horton's secret?

In *Dividing the Estate*:

> LEWIS: I thought you spoke eloquently at Doug's funeral . . . I
> wanted to speak, but I was too emotional—I didn't dare try.

and

> LUCILLE: I don't know what I had expected. Something much
> more emotional, I suppose.

Horton's people live on the brink of as much despair and ruin and loss as the people in any Williams or Miller play, and yet—and yet—it's as if Horton's people don't know they can be theatrical. They can make out the contours of their problem—but how to deal with it? Horton's people have no concept of self-dramatization. Is this Horton's dramatic secret: his characters don't know they're in a play? They don't know they have the luxury of license to behave in a more outsize way. Horton's people had a restraint, a decorum that reminded me of—do I go too far?—the abstract purity of a Racine!

In their plainspoken fashion, were they correctives to the legacy of Tennessee Williams? Not to diminish Tennessee Williams, whom I revere, but the great man had spawned a lot of bad imitators. And in the second part of his career, Tennessee was even accused of imitating himself. You can imitate Tennessee. You can't imitate Horton. Good God—could Horton Foote be the counterbalance, the yin to the yang of Tennessee Williams?

In the movie *Sunset Boulevard,* William Holden says to Gloria Swanson, "You used to be big." She replies, "I *am* big. It's the *pictures* that got small."

It was the opposite with Horton. I thought him small only because I had first seen him in black-and-white within the frame of a twelve-inch screen. I learned that, after he won his Oscar, instead of buying the place in Malibu, he moved his wife and four children from Nyack, New York, to New Hampshire, where he could write his plays in peace. He didn't care about commercial productions or current fads. He had some of his plays produced at HB Studio in Greenwich Village, with no admission charge. He wrote. That was enough.

So what did I learn from wandering into that dusty Chicago bookstore?

I found these words of Horton's:

> Take all the counsel and advice you can get, but remember, finally, it is you alone in a room with a blank piece of paper staring at you. How then can you know what advice to take and to whom to listen? That, too, is something you cannot be told. That is something every writer has to discover for himself. Sometimes writers are badly advised, they listen to that advice and are harmed. Yet, even then you are learning. Essentially what you are learning is who you are and how you are different from other writers. Cherish that difference, not in arrogance, but in humility and in gratitude that you are allowed such differences. For wouldn't it be awful if every talent was the same, if we all wrote alike?

I thought of the playwriting students I've had over the years who stride into class like mini-Tamburlaines clutching their pitch-perfect imitations of a Pinter play or a Mamet play or a Shepard play. That's not playwriting; that's ventriloquism. Listen to Horton: "The main task of a playwright is to find your own voice—that unique look at life which separates you from the pack. To find the emotional terrain that you make your own. A writer must write what he must write and damn the consequences." If I want to write mermaids, all I can do is write them as well and as honestly as I can. Horton's life is a paean to the joy of creation.

We have in this volume a mere three plays of Horton's vast output written over a span of more than sixty years. What's astonishing is the purity and unbroken continuity of Horton's voice. There don't seem to be any dry periods. There don't seem to be periods where Horton takes a wild stylistic turn and veers off course. He found his path early on and just stayed there. His plays do the magic that every writer dreams of—they transcend the time in which they were written. They speak directly to now.

He makes me think of Irving Berlin, who wrote an astonishing number of songs over as many years as Horton has been writing.

He makes me think of the American painter Chuck Close, whose obsession for nearly fifty years has been simply recording the landscape of the human face. Close needs no more nourishment than the human face to make his art.

Horton's obsession is the face of Harrison, Texas, and its environs.

Horton has created an alternate universe as fully and richly populated as the world of Anthony Trollope, who catalogued nineteenth-century English country life in over sixty hypnotic novels, with vivid characters like the Duke of Omnium and Lady Glencora Palliser crisscrossing in and out of Trollope's seemingly narrow canvas. I went from one novel to another. My wife said to me, "Did your parole officer say you could only read novels by Trollope?" But you get hooked into Trollope's universe.

Horton's Harrison, Texas, makes me think of Faulkner's Yoknapatawpha County. Someday some noble soul will make a directory of Horton's world and let us see the magnitude of all his interlinking lives.

Horton once quoted Matisse, who observed to Picasso, "In your painting you tear things apart and with me I put things together."

I was fifteen when Horton Foote first put things together for me in *A Young Lady of Property*. I found Horton and then lost Horton and then found him again. Good God—now I'm seventy. I write this introduction on March 14, 2008, which is the occasion of Horton's ninety-second birthday. Where is Horton on this venerable day? Doing what a playwright should be doing. He's in Chicago, where the Goodman Theater is presenting a festival of his plays. He's also back and forth to California trying to get his new screenplay off the ground. He's returning to New York soon for Lincoln Center's Broadway production of *Dividing the Estate*, which got the best reviews of last season when it was done off-Broadway. He has a few new plays in his typewriter.

Another reason for this seventy-year-old playwright to love him: Horton gives me the illusion that I'm only in midcareer.

Thank you, Horton.

THREE PLAYS

DIVIDING THE ESTATE

PRODUCTION HISTORY

Dividing the Estate was produced by Lincoln Center Theatre (Andre Bishop, artistic director, and Bernard Gersten, executive producer), by arrangement with Primary Stages (Casey Childs, founder and executive producer, Andrew Leynse, artistic director, and Elliot Fox, managing director), opening on November 20, 2008, at the Primary Stages Theatre. It was directed by Michael Wilson, with set design by Jeff Cowie, costume design by David C. Woolard, lighting design by Rui Rita, and original music and sound design by John Gromada. Cole Bonenberger was the production stage manager.

Son	Devon Abner
Stella Gordon	Elizabeth Ashley
Lucille	Penny Fuller
Mildred	Pat Bowie
Doug	Arthur French
Lewis Gordon	Gerald McRaney
Pauline	Maggie Lacey
Cathleen	Keiana Richard
Sissie	Nicole Lowrance
Emily	Jenny Dare Paulin
Mary Jo	Hallie Foote
Bob	James DeMarse
Irene Ratliff	Virginia Kull

CHARACTERS

Son
Stella Gordon
Lucille
Mildred
Doug
Lewis Gordon
Pauline
Cathleen
Sissie
Emily
Mary Jo
Bob
Irene Ratliff

ACT 1

SCENE 1

[*1987, Harrison, Texas. A living room in the Gordon house. It is an old-fashioned, comfortable room. Through double doors one can see the dining room with a table being set for dinner by three black servants, a man and two women. They appear and reappear at different times, setting the table, arranging flowers.*

SON *is alone in the room, reading a paper.* LUCILLE *and* STELLA *enter.* LUCILLE, *a noticeably nervous woman, has* STELLA *by the arms.* SON *rises when they enter.*]

SON: Grandmother, here—take your chair.

STELLA: No, Son, I'll sit over here.

LUCILLE: Now, Mama, Son doesn't mind you having that chair. He knows it's where you always sit.

[SON *goes to* STELLA *and leads her to the chair he was sitting in.* MILDRED, *one of the black women, comes into the room.*]

MILDRED: How many coming for dinner?

LUCILLE: Let's see . . . Mama and me and Son and Brother, and . . .

STELLA: Where is Brother?

LUCILLE: I don't know. I haven't seen him since breakfast. Go see if you can find him, Sonny. Tell him Mama was asking for him.

SON: Yes, ma'am.

[SON *goes.*]

MILDRED: You still haven't answered my question, Miss Lucille. How many are coming to dinner?

LUCILLE: Well, let's see. There are the four of us, and Sister and her two children, and Bob . . .

STELLA: Are Mary Jo's girls bringing their husbands?

LUCILLE: No, Mama. Heavens, they are both divorced. Now, you remember that.

STELLA: I don't remember it at all.

LUCILLE: My God, Mama. Of course you do. Sissie divorced her husband last fall, and Mary Jo and Bob had Emily's marriage annulled a week after she was married.

STELLA: Did they marry boys from here?

LUCILLE: No, they were both Houston boys.

STELLA: Were they well connected?

LUCILLE: Who?

STELLA: The boys my granddaughters married.

LUCILLE: They were both lazy and no-good, according to Mary Jo and Bob, but they came from lovely families.

STELLA: Which child was it had that awful tragedy the night of her wedding?

LUCILLE: I don't know what you are talking about, Mama.

STELLA: Yes, you do, too. One of the girls' husbands blew his brains out on their wedding night.

LUCILLE: No, Mama. That wasn't Sissie or Emily's husband.

STELLA: Whose husband was it?

LUCILLE: That was Cousin Gert Stewart's daughter's husband—I forget her name.

STELLA: Clara Belle?

LUCILLE: No, that's the oldest girl.

STELLA: Catherine Lee?

LUCILLE: Yes, she is the one.

STELLA: Why did that happen? Did he leave a note?

LUCILLE: No. Gert just said it was an accident.

STELLA: An accident?

LUCILLE: Yes—that he was cleaning his gun, and he was laughing, and he said, "If I didn't think you loved me, I'd kill myself," and the gun accidentally went off, and she ran to him screaming and held him, and blood was running all over her beautiful wedding gown—you remember, that wedding gown had been in Gert's family for generations. Her great-great-grandmother had brought it with her from Virginia.

STELLA: What was he doing cleaning his gun on his wedding night?

LUCILLE: No one knows, Mama. That is just one of those great mysteries.

STELLA: Wasn't Miss Pauline invited for dinner?

LUCILLE: Oh, yes. That's right.

MILDRED: And that will make nine.

LUCILLE: Yes.

[MILDRED *starts away*.]

Mildred . . .

MILDRED: Yes'm.

LUCILLE: You had better set ten places, just in case. I keep thinking I've invited someone else.

MILDRED: You probably invited five more, if I know you.

LUCILLE: Oh, I hope not. Well, we always have plenty of food, that's one thing.

MILDRED: Mr. Son is after me about the grocery bills again. I said, "Mr. Son, I don't make up the menu. Speak to your mama."

STELLA: There is only one way to economize, and that's to have a garden and grow your own vegetables.

[DOUG, *an old black man, comes into the dining room*.]

Kill your own hogs, have a cow and calves and chickens. There is no reason why this place can't be self-sufficient again.

LUCILLE: My God, Mama—be sensible. We're living in the middle of the town on a highway. You can't keep pigs and chickens and cows here now.

STELLA: Doug . . .

DOUG: Yes, ma'am.

STELLA: Come in here.

DOUG: Yes, ma'am.

[DOUG *enters into the living room*.]

STELLA: I want you to put in a garden again. I want you to get some pigs, and some chickens and cows . . .

DOUG: Miss Stella, I'm an old man. I can't do that anymore.

STELLA: Well, find somebody who can.

DOUG: You can't find people to do work like that no more, Miss Stella. And if you find them, you couldn't afford their wages.

STELLA: How old are you, Doug?

DOUG: Ninety-two.

STELLA: When did you come to work here?

DOUG: When I was five years old. Your papa brought my mama in from the farm after my daddy was killed by one of the bulls, and she cooked for you all.

STELLA: Henrietta?

DOUG: Yes'm. I remember the day you was born and the day you got married, and the day your husband, Mister Charles, died.

STELLA: Charlie wasn't my husband, Doug. He was Lucille's husband— Donald was my husband.

DOUG: Yes'm that's how it was. I remember all of it.

[DOUG *leaves.* MILDRED *leaves.*]

STELLA: Did I hear you say Pauline is coming?

LUCILLE: Yes.

STELLA: Who invited her?

LUCILLE: Son.

STELLA: You know, I have never understood why our young men here are always attracted to schoolteachers. Do you realize how many of the young men here married schoolteachers? Both the Courtney boys, Mr. Jackson, Lewis Fraley—oh, there are so many.

[*Pause.*]

Miss Pauline's very modern, I think. She's always giving lectures. I cannot stand the way she lectures you. She thinks she knows the answer to everything—why we no longer find it profitable to grow cotton here, why the chemical plants are poisoning our environment here on the Coast, why the Mexicans are coming in droves from Mexico, why . . .

LUCILLE: Well, Mama, I find her very sensible and down-to-earth. And personally I'm grateful Son has found someone like Pauline, after all he went through with his first wife.

STELLA: Why do you think Olive Louise divorced Son?

LUCILLE: Now, Mama, we've been over this a thousand times, and you know very well I don't know the answer to that.

STELLA: Why does Son think she did?

LUCILLE: I don't know. We've never discussed it with him. All I know was he was very hurt and upset.

STELLA: I'm going to ask him.

LUCILLE: Don't you dare.

STELLA: I'd certainly like to know. Maybe one day I'll ask Olive Louise.

LUCILLE: You can't ask her, Mama. She's dead. Heavens!

STELLA: Oh, that's right. She certainly is. Bless her heart. She was on her way to the airport with a drunken man and they had a wreck. Where were they off to?

LUCILLE: Who?

STELLA: Olive Louise and the drunken man.

LUCILLE: I don't know, Mama. I never heard.

STELLA: I heard New York City to see some plays. Well, I wish someone would tell Pauline to stop acting like an encyclopedia.

LUCILLE: Oh, Mama, the poor thing has to talk about something. All we ever talk about is our family and friends. That must be very boring to her. This is not her family and these are not her friends.

STELLA: Doesn't she have any family?

LUCILLE: Of course she does, Mama, but if she talked about them, we wouldn't know who in the world she was talking about.

STELLA: I don't care for overeducated women. I never have.

[LEWIS *enters—he is* STELLA's *son and* LUCILLE's *brother.*]

LUCILLE: Did Son find you?

LEWIS: No.

LUCILLE: He went looking for you.

STELLA: Where were you?

LEWIS: I took a walk downtown.

STELLA: Lewis . . .

LEWIS: Yes, Mama.

STELLA: I smell liquor on your breath. Have you been drinking?

LEWIS: Yes, Mama.

STELLA: So early in the morning?

LEWIS: Yes, Mama.

STELLA: I don't allow liquor in this house.

LEWIS: I know that, Mama. I don't drink it in this house.

[DOUG *has reappeared in the dining room.*]

DOUG: Miss Ida Belle Coons was a Coke fiend. She drank Coca-Colas all day long.

LEWIS: Nobody wants to hear about Ida Belle Coons, Doug.

DOUG: Mrs. Coons's cook told us that Mrs. Coons banned Coca-Colas from the house, but Miss Ida Belle would slip out of the house and go over to the Texaco filling station and buy her Cokes. The cook said she would slip out at seven in the morning and be there waiting for the filling station to open.

STELLA: Merciful God.

DOUG: Coca-Colas are bad for you if you drink too many. Mr. Leroy had the lining of his stomach eaten out from drinking Coca-Colas, everybody says.

STELLA: That's the truth . . .

DOUG: And I tell you another thing . . .

LEWIS: All right Doug, that's enough.

DOUG: Yessir. You know I can read and write and do the multiplication tables—your mama taught me. I never went to school, but your mama did, and she say to me—she wasn't more than twelve—"How old are you?" "Twenty-two," I say. "And you can't read or write?" "No, ma'am," I says. "Then I'm going to teach you," she says, and she did. I knows all the books in the Bible—Genesis, Exodus . . .

LEWIS: All right, Doug. We know you do.

DOUG: I read in the Bible every morning and every night.

LEWIS: Hush up, Doug.

DOUG: Do you read your Bible?

LEWIS: I said hush up, Doug.

[DOUG *leaves.*]

STELLA: Lewis, you promised me.

LEWIS: I know, Mama, but I've broken my promise.

STELLA: Why?

LEWIS: Because I am very nervous today.

[*Pause.*]

I wanted to go on record as saying I am for immediately dividing the estate.

STELLA: Why?

LEWIS: Because . . .

STELLA: You would run through your share in a day . . .

LEWIS: Then I'll run through it.

[SON *enters.*]

But I'm tired of having pittances doled out to me by my nephew every month.

STELLA: Pittances. You have a house, three wonderful meals every day. Servants to wait on you hand and foot, four hundred dollars every month, a car . . .

[MILDRED *reappears.*]

MILDRED: Miss Lucille, did you tell Doug he couldn't serve the food today?

LUCILLE: Not yet—

MILDRED: Well, you better tell him. He's bound and determined. I told him Cathleen was going to serve, and he said he'd break both of her arms if she tried.

STELLA: Why can't Doug serve?

LUCILLE: Because his hands shake and tremble, Mama. He spilled gravy all over Miss Mary Cox last time she was here for dinner.

[DOUG *comes out, followed by* CATHLEEN.]

DOUG: Miss Stella, this fresh thing says she is going to serve your dinner today and not me. You tell her she is wrong.

LUCILLE: She's not wrong, Doug. We've retired you now, you know that.

DOUG: I don't want to be retired.

LUCILLE: Well, you are, so be quiet.

STELLA: Don't talk to Doug that way, Lucille.

LUCILLE: Please, Mama—

STELLA: I want him to serve the dinner.

LUCILLE: Mama, how—

STELLA: I said he's going to serve that dinner.

LUCILLE: All right, Mama. Cathleen, let him have his way.

[DOUG *and* CATHLEEN *go back to the kitchen.*]

SON [*singing to himself*]: "Rock of ages, Cleft for me . . ."

STELLA: Why are you singing that, Son?

SON: I don't know, it just came into my head, so I sang it.

STELLA: Is this teacher you go with religious?

SON: Yes, I think she is. She is no fanatic. She's not there every time the church doors open, but she goes to church.

STELLA: Which one?

SON: Methodist.

STELLA: Does she know you are a Baptist?

SON: Yes.

STELLA: Of course, in my day that was a very serious matter if one was a Baptist and one was Methodist. Now, of course, it doesn't seem to matter. Baptists marry anybody and anything—Methodists, Catholics, Lutherans, Holy Rollers . . .

LEWIS: I just love the way everybody in this family changes subjects. I made a statement earlier about dividing the estate.

STELLA: That's just because you've been drinking, Lewis. That's how you always talk when you're drinking.

LEWIS: I am sick and tired of having to go to my nephew for the least thing. Son, I need ten dollars or fifteen or twenty. Why? Because I spent my allowance too soon this month. Why? Because it is none of your goddamned business is why.

STELLA: Lewis, Lewis, just shut up. Shut up if you have to talk that way. Thank God we have Son, is all I say. Thank God Son is willing to devote his life to keep this estate in operation. This estate has taken very good care of us all these years, hasn't it? It took care of my mother and father, me and my family. It took care of my grandfather and grandmother.

LEWIS: These are difficult times. Cotton is too expensive to grow these days.

STELLA: Don't talk to me about difficult times. We got through the Depression, when people were abandoning their land, selling it all over this country, but my father held on to our land, scraped together the money to plant cotton every year, pay our taxes, and keep body and soul together. Just look at what is surrounding us. Fruit markets and fast-food restaurants. That's what happens when you sell your land. Of course, the sight of all that squalor is all you've ever known,

Son, but when your mother and uncle were growing up, this was a
lovely, quiet street. Beautiful homes—

LUCILLE: Son knows that, Mama—

STELLA: Fine, gracious, lovely homes.

LEWIS: People sold because they needed money.

STELLA: Too bad.

[*Pause.*]

I'm not feeling well. I'm going to my room.

LUCILLE: Now, Mama. Mama, please don't go—you're going to spoil
everything.

STELLA: I know what you're all up to. Plotting behind my back. The
minute I'm dead you'll sell this house, divide the land, and it will all
be gone. Well, you'll never do it while I'm alive. I tell you that.

[STELLA *leaves.*]

LUCILLE: Brother, why in the world—

[*Pause.*]

My God, my God.

LEWIS: I need some money.

SON: For what?

LEWIS: Never mind. I just need money—

SON: Uncle, I've already given you two advances, you know.

LEWIS: It's not your money.

SON: I'm aware of that.

LEWIS: Then just give it to me and shut up.

SON: How much do you want?

LEWIS: A large sum.

SON: How much?

LEWIS: You can deduct it from my share of the estate.

SON: How much, Uncle Lewis?

LEWIS: Ten thousand dollars.

SON: Ten thousand dollars! My God, Uncle Lewis, the estate can't afford
shelling out money like that.

LEWIS: You're not giving me anything—I said to take it off my share of
the estate.

SON: I gave you fifteen thousand dollars last year.

LEWIS: You gave me nothing—I took it out of my share of the estate.

SON: Do you know how much you already owe the estate?

LEWIS: No, but I bet you do.

SON: You're goddamned right I do.

LUCILLE: Son . . . Son . . .

SON: Two hundred thousand dollars.

LEWIS: I don't believe it.

SON: It's there in black and white.

LEWIS: How much has Mary Jo taken?

SON: Plenty.

LEWIS: How much?

SON: I can't tell you offhand.

[*Pause.*]

LEWIS: Just don't argue and give me the ten thousand dollars.

SON: I'm not going to do it. Not until the end of the year and we can see how we stand. I may have to borrow money to pay the taxes again.

LEWIS: Goddamn it, it's my money.

[PAULINE *enters.*]

PAULINE: Good morning. I hope I'm not late.

SON: No, our Houston kin aren't here yet.

PAULINE: What a day—what a lovely day!

LUCILLE: Yes, it is.

PAULINE: I was over at the Historical Museum just now looking for some pictures of the town for an article I'm writing for the *Houston Post.* I had never seen pictures of this street before they paved it. It was simply beautiful. It's too bad that so many of the lovely old houses have been torn down. I'm glad you've saved this one. Have you heard about the restoration plan for our town?

LUCILLE: I've heard something about it.

PAULINE: This could be a beautiful town, you know, if the buildings were restored.

[*She laughs.*]

Oh, well. Son, I'm sure, is tired of hearing me go on about this.

LUCILLE: Are they busy uptown?

PAULINE: No, it's very quiet.

LUCILLE: It used to be so busy in town on Saturdays, and so crowded you could hardly walk down the sidewalk.

LEWIS: Are you going to give me the money, Son?

SON: I can't now, Uncle.

LEWIS: I want it now.

SON: You can't have it now.

LEWIS: I want to have it now.

PAULINE: Maybe I should go . . .

SON: No, stay. This goes on all the time.

LEWIS: Jesus Christ, you sonofabitch.

[LEWIS *gets up and starts out.*]

LUCILLE: Lewis . . .

LEWIS: Go to hell. I'm going to a lawyer and have those books examined. I want to see just how much I do owe. I don't trust your son, lady.

[LEWIS *goes.*]

LUCILLE: Excuse me.

[LUCILLE *goes.*]

SON: Don't get upset over anything he says—he's been drinking. He can be a terror when he's drinking. And he wants money. You see, he gambles. He's a terrible gambler and so he always loses, and he gets into debt and then he has to borrow from the estate to pay his debts.

PAULINE: Does he have a job?

SON: No.

PAULINE: Has he ever had a job?

SON: One or two. But then he'd get on a drunk and get fired.

PAULINE: Does he help you out at the farms?

SON: No. He tried managing them right after my grandfather died, but he got things so screwed up that my grandmother took everything away from him and asked my father to take over.

PAULINE: He's never married?

SON: No. He's had plenty of lady friends, but none the family felt he should marry.

PAULINE: The family?

SON: My grandmother and grandfather.

PAULINE: What was wrong with them?

SON: Well, you know Miss Pearl Davis?

PAULINE: Yes.

SON: She was one of them.

PAULINE: What's wrong with her?

SON: They thought she was after his money. And I've heard about the others. I never knew them.

[DOUG *comes out.*]

DOUG: Son, I have to lie down.

SON: All right, Doug.

DOUG: Those women out in the kitchen are trying to conjure me.

[MILDRED *comes out.*]

MILDRED: Mr. Son, don't believe a word he says—he's just old and mean.

DOUG: She and Cathleen been conjuring me, Son. They won't rest until I'm dead.

MILDRED: You ought to be ashamed of yourself talking that way— nobody is studying you, old man. Nobody in this world. Cathleen is crying out there because of your foolishness. You have her so upset, old man, with all this conjure talk, she is a nervous wreck. Mr. Son, make him behave, and come talk to Cathleen.

SON: All right. You go on back to the kitchen and tell Cathleen I'll be right out.

[MILDRED *goes.*]

Come on, Doug. Let's go lie down and rest—you'll feel better.

DOUG: You know what they say to me? They say I talk ignorant. That I'm old-timey.

SON: Don't worry about it. Now, come on.

DOUG: Cathleen think she so smart because she goes to the Junior College. I couldn't go to any Junior College. They didn't have no Junior College when I was coming along. They say I wouldn't have gone anyway, because I'm too ignorant. I said I would have gone. I can read and write and do the multiplication tables, and they say that ain't nothing at all. Anybody can do that. Not when I was coming along, they couldn't.

SON: I know, I know, now don't get any more upset than you are—come on, now. Doug, it's not good for you to get upset. Come on.

[CATHLEEN *and* MILDRED *come out.*]

CATHLEEN: I've been listening to every word you've said, old man. Nobody is making fun of you. You're the one making fun of people, saying I'm crazy, trying to go to college. Saying I'm forgetting my place—saying—

SON: All right, Cathleen. All right.

[CATHLEEN *cries.*]

CATHLEEN: He talks so mean to me, Mr. Son. He talks so mean to me all the time.

MILDRED: You know what he told her? He told her her daddy is going to end up in the electric chair.

DOUG: No, I did not say that.

MILDRED: Yes you did.

DOUG: What I said is that they got him locked up over at the Retrieve Plantation, and if he cuts another man, they'll send him to Huntsville next time, and then the electric chair.

CATHLEEN: You see, you see, Mr. Son.

DOUG [*he is yelling now*]: Your daddy is no good and you know he is no good.

SON: All right, Doug.

DOUG: He beats you and your mama.

SON: Just be quiet now.

DOUG: He cut that woman he was living with until she near about died.

SON: Cathleen, pay no attention to him.

DOUG: He cut three men, one of them white.

CATHLEEN: Pay no attention to him? He follows me around all the time saying I'm trying to take his job.

DOUG: You're trying to get my job through conjure.

CATHLEEN: Shut up, you ignorant old man. Nobody believes in conjure anymore, except ignorant old fools like you. Just shut up.

[DOUG *faints and falls to the floor.*]

MILDRED [*screams*]: Oh, Jesus—oh, Jesus.
CATHLEEN [*screams*]: God have mercy!

[SON *goes to him.*]

SON: Doug, Doug . . .

[*He turns to* PAULINE.]

    Pauline, call Dr. Anderson.
PAULINE: All right.

[PAULINE *goes,* CATHLEEN *cries.*]

SON: Sh, Cathleen. Mildred, just take her into the kitchen.

[LUCILLE *is heard calling "Mildred, Mildred."*]

MILDRED: Yes'm.
LUCILLE [*offstage*]: Where are you?
MILDRED: In the living room.
LUCILLE [*offstage*]: Who's that crying? What's going on?
MILDRED: It's Cathleen—

[LUCILLE *comes in.*]

LUCILLE: What on earth—what has happened?
SON: Cathleen had her feelings hurt by Doug.
LUCILLE: What's wrong with Doug?
SON: I don't know. He got excited and passed out.

[LUCILLE *goes to* DOUG.]

LUCILLE: Doug—Doug.
DOUG: Yes'm, who's that? Oh, Miss Lucille.

[DOUG *sits up.*]

SON: Doug, lie down until the doctor gets here.
DOUG: What doctor?
SON: Dr. Anderson. Pauline has gone to call him.
DOUG: I don't need any doctor. I'm all right. Help me up, Son.

SON: Are you sure?

DOUG: Yes, I'm sure.

[SON *helps* DOUG *up.* DOUG *points to* CATHLEEN.]

What's wrong with her?

MILDRED: You know what's wrong with her—your devilish ways is what's wrong with her.

[CATHLEEN *cries.*]

LUCILLE: Now, Cathleen, Cathleen.

[LUCILLE *goes to her.*]

Let's all keep calm—our company will be here soon.

CATHLEEN: Miss Lucille, I can't work no more today. I'm too nervous to work. I'm just too nervous.

LUCILLE: Well, all right. Son, will you drive her home?

SON: Come on, Cathleen.

[PAULINE *enters.*]

PAULINE: The doctor says to bring him to the hospital right away.

SON: He doesn't need to go to the hospital now. He says he is feeling all right.

DOUG: Just get the conjure out of the house. I'll be all right.

[CATHLEEN *begins to cry again.*]

LUCILLE: Cathleen . . .

MILDRED: Tell him to shut his mouth, Miss Lucille. He accuses Cathleen of conjuring him, and that is a lie.

SON: Come on, Cathleen. Just don't pay any attention—he's an old man.

CATHLEEN [*wiping her eyes*]: Let me get my things.

[CATHLEEN *goes out to the kitchen.*]

SON: Pauline and I will meet you out at the car.

[SON *and* PAULINE *leave.* MILDRED *goes.* DOUG *has fallen asleep in his chair.*]

LUCILLE: Doug . . . Doug . . .

[DOUG *is asleep.* LUCILLE *goes into the kitchen.* LEWIS *comes in.*]

LEWIS [*calling*]: Sister . . . Sister . . .

[LUCILLE *comes back in.*]

LUCILLE: Sh . . . sh . . . Doug is asleep. He's not feeling well. Cathleen
    had to go home. I'm doing what I can do to help Mildred—we're hav-
    ing nine for dinner.
LEWIS: I have to have that money, Sister. Will you tell Son that?
LUCILLE: I can't interfere about that, Brother.

[DOUG *wakes up.*]

DOUG: Who is here?
LUCILLE: Just me and Lewis, Doug. How do you feel?
DOUG: I feel fine. Who says I didn't?
LUCILLE: Why don't you go in the kitchen now and see if you can help
    Mildred? She's all alone out there.
DOUG: I'm serving the meal today?
LUCILLE: Yes, you are serving the meal today.

[DOUG *closes his eyes and goes back to sleep.*]

STELLA [*entering*]: Lucille.
LUCILLE: Yes, Mama.
STELLA: I wonder where Mary Jo and her family are? They're late.
LUCILLE: No, they're not late, Mama.

[LEWIS *leaves the room.*]

STELLA: Doug is asleep. I don't want him asleep in here when Mary Jo
    and her family arrive.
LUCILLE: I'll wake him when I hear their car drive up.
STELLA: How long has Son's wife been dead?
LUCILLE: Let's see . . .

[*Pause.*]

    A year. Is it possible?
STELLA: How long after she left Son was she killed?

LUCILLE: Let's see . . .

[*Pause.*]

Three months.

STELLA: Was she drunk when she had the accident?

LUCILLE: No, she was not drunk, Mother—heavens. The man she was with was drunk, they say. We don't know for sure.

STELLA: That was God's punishment to her for leaving Son and going out with other men.

LUCILLE: Now, Mama, you know God doesn't punish people for things like that by killing them.

STELLA: He certainly does.

LUCILLE: Well, then that's not a God I care to know about.

STELLA: He's a vengeful God, you know, punishing sinners.

LUCILLE: All right, Mama, if you say so. Was Charlie a sinner?

STELLA: No, Charlie wasn't a sinner.

LUCILLE: He certainly wasn't a sinner—all he did was slave for this family.

STELLA: That's right—morning, noon, and night.

LUCILLE: Then why was he struck down, slaving away out at the farms for us?

STELLA: I don't know about that . . .

LUCILLE: Well, I can tell you, my husband was not a sinner. He was a good, kind man.

STELLA: Your father was a sinner—he fathered children all up and down this county, black and white. I warned him he'd be struck down right in a bed of iniquity, but he never was. He died just as peaceful . . .

LUCILLE: He didn't die peaceful, Mama. He was in great pain when he died.

STELLA: Well, he was in his own bed being cared for by his family. I despised him, you know.

LUCILLE: Mama, don't say that.

STELLA: I did. I despised him. I would've left him, too, except for you children.

LUCILLE: Why did you marry him, Mama? Didn't you know his ways?

STELLA: I was worried about them, but I was young and innocent and he was handsome, and I was flattered by his attention because he was known as such a good catch. I felt surely I could reform him. But I couldn't . . .

[*Pause.* LEWIS *comes in.*]

LEWIS: Mama . . .

STELLA: Yes.

LEWIS: I have to borrow some money from the estate.

STELLA: My God, Lewis. You have asked me that four times today. And I have told you four times that I will not give you any more money.

LEWIS: Mama . . .

STELLA: Lewis . . .

LEWIS: It's life or death, Mama.

STELLA: Life or death?

LEWIS: Yes.

STELLA: Did you hear that, Lucille?

LUCILLE: Yes.

STELLA: You're not lying to me, Lewis?

LEWIS: No, Mama.

STELLA: Tell me why it is life or death—

LEWIS: I can't, Mama.

STELLA: Can you tell Lucille?

LEWIS: No.

STELLA: Can you tell Son?

LEWIS: Yes.

STELLA: Why can't you tell me?

LEWIS: Because I am ashamed to, Mama.

STELLA: Ashamed?

LEWIS: Yes.

[SON *comes in with* PAULINE.]

SON: Hello.

STELLA: Son, give Lewis the money he needs.

SON: Ten thousand dollars?

STELLA: Yes, if that's what he needs.

SON: But Grandmother, we can't spare that money right now—I was explaining to Uncle Lewis . . .

STELLA: Well, you'll sell something then, Son. He says it's life or death—

SON: What do you want me to sell?

STELLA: Use your own judgment.

LEWIS: I need the money now, Son.

SON: Right now?

LEWIS: Yes, right now.

SON: All right—come on down to the bank and I'll see what I can arrange.

STELLA: He's going to tell you why he needs it, Son.

SON: That is really no concern of mine.

STELLA: I want him to tell you.

SON: All right.

[SON *and* LEWIS *leave.*]

STELLA: Lucille . . .

LUCILLE: Yes, Mama.

STELLA: Do you believe it's life or death?

LUCILLE: I don't know, Mama.

[DOUG *wakes up.*]

DOUG [*singing*]: "Rock of Ages, Cleft for me . . ."

STELLA: Why are you singing that hymn, Doug? Son was singing it this morning, too. I don't care for that hymn, you know—I never have.

LUCILLE: They sang it at Papa's funeral.

STELLA: Did they? Well, I forbid them to sing it at mine.

DOUG: You won't know what they're singing at your funeral.

STELLA: If either of you are around, tell them not to.

DOUG: I want it sung at my funeral. [*He sings*] "Rock of Ages, Cleft for me . . ."

STELLA: Hush up, Doug, it's not your funeral now.

DOUG: I want you to promise me one thing: that they will sing "Rock of Ages" as they're lowering my coffin into the grave and that you'll buy me a nice tombstone.

STELLA: I have already promised you that a million times—so has Lucille, and so has Son.

[MILDRED *comes to the kitchen door.*]

MILDRED: I need some help out in the kitchen. I can't do all the work myself.

LUCILLE: I'm going to help you, Mildred.

[LUCILLE *gets up and goes into the kitchen.*]

STELLA: You go help her too, Doug.

DOUG: No, thank you. I'm tired. I'm going to set here and rest until it's time to serve your dinner.

[*He closes his eyes.*]

STELLA [*singing half to herself*]: "Rock of Ages, Cleft for me . . ."

[*Pause.*]

I hate that damn hymn.

[*She closes her eyes.*]

DOUG: Fine tombstone and a fine coffin.

STELLA: We've promised you that, too, so be quiet. You know why Mary Jo and her husband are coming to pay me a visit?

DOUG: Because they're lonesome for you.

STELLA: No, indeed. Because they need money—and I bet you anything I have they won't be here for five minutes before Mary Jo will be nagging me about dividing the estate.

[*Pause.*]

I'm never going to divide it, Doug.

DOUG: Yes'm.

STELLA: She can beg and beg, and Lewis can beg and beg. I'm never in this world going to divide it.

DOUG: If you divide it, who gets the house out back I live in?

STELLA: I'm never going to divide it—never.

DOUG: Well, I'm glad to hear that. I'm too old now to move from my house.

[*Pause.*]

Miss Stella—

STELLA: Yes?

DOUG: I want you to promise me one more thing.

STELLA: What's that?

DOUG: When I die . . .

STELLA: Yes, I know you want a tombstone.

DOUG: Something more—when I die, I want you to bury me next to my mama's grave.

STELLA: I forget, does she have a tombstone?

DOUG: No, she don't.

STELLA: How will I find her grave?

DOUG: I'll go out there tomorrow and show it to you. I keeps red flowers in a Mason jar on it.

STELLA: What kind of red flowers are they, Doug?

DOUG: No kind. They're paper.

STELLA: I see.

[*She closes her eyes.*]

DOUG: You'll go out there with me tomorrow?

STELLA: I will.

[DOUG *closes his eyes. They are soon asleep as the lights fade.*]

SCENE 2

[*Later the same day.* MARY JO *is there looking around the room.* MILDRED *comes in.*]

MILDRED: Good Lord a mercy, look who's here. Mary Jo, as I live and breathe. Where are the girls?

MARY JO: They're upstairs visiting with Mama.

MILDRED: I know she's glad to see them.

MARY JO: I think so.

MILDRED: How long since you've been here?

MARY JO: It's been at least five months, Mildred.

MILDRED: When you coming back to stay?

MARY JO [*laughs*]: Oh, I don't know darling. I'm a Houston girl now.

[EMILY *and* SISSIE *come in.*]

Mildred, do you remember these girls?

MILDRED: No, Lord. They have grown.

SISSIE: Grandma kept calling me Emily and Emily Sissie.

MARY JO: Girls, how long since we've been here? Five months or six?

EMILY: Grandma said Thanksgiving, but it wasn't Thanksgiving. We went to College Station for the football game.

MILDRED: Well, you both look mighty fine.

[LUCILLE *comes in.*]

LUCILLE: Where is Bob?

MARY JO: He'll be along. When we were driving through town on our way home he saw Carson Davis and stopped off to visit with him.

LUCILLE: We have a plastic factory here now, you know.

MARY JO: A plastic factory?

LUCILLE: Yes. We had a mattress factory about six years ago, but it didn't seem to prosper.

MARY JO: Who owns the plastic factory? Anyone we know?

LUCILLE: No. It's owned by a man from Taiwan.

MARY JO: Taiwan? My God, how did he ever get here?

LUCILLE: I don't know. They're all over the coast fishing.

MARY JO: They're not from Taiwan, Sister—they're from Vietnam.

LUCILLE: Oh.

MARY JO: I'm going to check on Mama. I'll bet she's forgotten we're here.

[MARY JO *goes.*]

LUCILLE: Your mama tells me you have serious beaux.

EMILY: Sissie has. I did have one for about two weeks.

LUCILLE: What happened?

EMILY: He turned out to be obnoxious.

SISSIE: Mama says Son is going with a schoolteacher.

LUCILLE: Yes.

EMILY: Do you approve?

LUCILLE: I certainly would like to see him marry again, if she's the right girl.

EMILY: Sometimes I don't think I'll ever marry again, all I went through with my husband. Mama gets furious when I say that. She says, "Look at Son, all he went through, and he's not bitter at all."

SISSIE: You know, she talked terribly about you all in Houston.

LUCILLE: Who did?

SISSIE: Olive Louise.

EMILY: She said you all had broken up her marriage. She said you and Uncle Lewis were weak, and Grandmother was domineering and tightfisted, and Son was no better than her slave. She said if she had to have another meal with you all in this house, she would have gone raving crazy.

LUCILLE: Who told you all this?

EMILY: Mama. She heard it someplace.

LUCILLE: Why didn't she ever tell me this?

EMILY: I don't know.

[MARY JO *enters.*]

LUCILLE: Mary Jo, why didn't you tell me about all these terrible things Olive Louise said about us in Houston before she died?

MARY JO: Who told you anything about that?

LUCILLE: Emily and Sissie.

MARY JO: Emily and Sissie, I told you not to repeat all that to your Aunt Lucille.

EMILY: No, you didn't.

MARY JO: I did, too. I most certainly did. I said I'm going to tell you something, but you must never repeat it to your Aunt Lucille.

LUCILLE: Why didn't you want it repeated to me?

MARY JO: Because I'm not even sure she said it.

LUCILLE: Who told you she said it?

MARY JO: Betty Grace Purcell.

LUCILLE: Who is that?

MARY JO: Someone I play bridge with once in a while in Houston.

LUCILLE: Did she say Olive Louise told that to her?

MARY JO: No.

LUCILLE: How did she hear it?

MARY JO: From Glen Eyrie Crawford.

LUCILLE: Who is that?

MARY JO: A third cousin of Olive Louise.

[STELLA *enters.*]

STELLA: What's this about Olive Louise?

LUCILLE: Nothing, Mama.

STELLA: Well, don't tell me. I know all about it, anyway—Lewis told me when he was mad at me this morning. He said she wouldn't come back to Son until the estate was divided. Well, I said, "Tell her that she'll never come back, because this estate won't be divided until hell freezes over."

LUCILLE: Olive Louise is dead, Mama. Heavens . . .

MARY JO: I think the estate should be divided. I agree with Olive Louise.

STELLA: Of course you do, Mary Jo, so you could throw it all away on trips to Europe and cars and expensive clothes. You wouldn't have a dime left after two months. Do you know how much you already borrowed from the estate?

MARY JO: No, and I don't want to know.

STELLA: Three hundred thousand dollars.

MARY JO: How do you know?

STELLA: Because I look at the books. I know every penny that is spent, and don't you forget it.

MARY JO: How much has Lewis borrowed?

STELLA: Two hundred thousand.

MARY JO: You mean I've borrowed three hundred thousand and Lewis has only borrowed two hundred thousand?

STELLA: Yes.

MARY JO: I find that hard to believe. All the money he's lost gambling, all the scrapes you've had to get him out of.

STELLA: Look at the books—it's all there. I told Doug not an hour ago you would begin on that the minute you got here. And I told Lucille the same thing . . .

LUCILLE: Now, Mama, you didn't say anything like that to me.

STELLA: I did, too. You said you absolutely agreed with me. You said she never came here unless she wanted something.

LUCILLE: Mama . . .

MARY JO: Thanks a lot, Lucille.

LUCILLE: Mary Jo, I did not say a single word of that.

MARY JO: How much has Lucille borrowed? And Son?

STELLA: Very little; two years for Son's college, and the money to bury Charlie.

MARY JO: What about them living here and eating here? I think they should be charged for that.

STELLA: Son works here, you know. Son takes care of all of this so you can borrow. If it weren't for Son . . .

MARY JO: Listen, I know all about Son—you don't have to tell me about Son. I appreciate Son just as much as you do. But do you mean to tell me that if Bob and Sissie and Emily and I come here to live that you wouldn't charge us for board and room?

STELLA: Certainly not. Not if you worked.

MARY JO: Well, I think we'll just move in this week. It would save us all a lot of money.

EMILY: Mama, let's change the subject.

MARY JO: All right, the subject's changed.

[BOB *enters.*]

BOB: Hello, Sister-in-Law.

LUCILLE: Hello, Bob.

BOB: You're looking well, Mother-in-Law—nothing much has changed around here, pretty as ever, but I can't say as much for the town, it's dying on the vine. I must have counted twenty-five empty stores.

LUCILLE: We're having a hard time. Houston is, too.

BOB: You can say that again. I know more people in Houston whose income was between seventy-five thousand and a hundred thousand dollars . . .

STELLA: How much?

BOB: Between seventy-five and a hundred thousand—paying off homes of a hundred or a hundred-fifty thousand dollars, with two kids in college, two cars, and suddenly the husband loses his job, and they lose everything, house, cars—now, this isn't just happening to one or two men but hundreds in the city of Houston.

[SON *and* PAULINE *enter.*]

SON: Hello. Pauline, this is my aunt and uncle, Mary Jo and Bob, and my cousins, Emily and Sissie.

PAULINE: How do you do—

MARY JO: Hello.

BOB: Hi, young lady—

[MILDRED *enters.*]

MILDRED: Can Doug serve your dinner now?

STELLA: We are waiting for Lewis.

SON: Uncle won't be here for dinner.

STELLA: Why?

SON: I don't know. When I left him at the bank, he said to tell you not to wait dinner.

BOB: Then let's eat.

STELLA: I'm not hungry—I'm going to my room.

MARY JO: Now, Mama, why are you going to spoil it for us?

STELLA: I'm not hungry. And I'm going to my room.

[STELLA *leaves.*]

MARY JO: Oh, I could wring Brother's neck. Well, this is the last time I'm coming fifty-five miles to eat a meal here, and have it spoiled because Brother gets on a drunk.

SON: Bob, Mary Jo, Mama . . . I think it's more than a drunk. He's in real trouble.

MARY JO: What in the name of God is it this time?

SON: He's been fooling around with a high school girl, and I don't know all the details. He was agitated when he told me about it. It seems her father has found out and threatened to kill him, and then he was told if he got money to him, the father would forget it. Uncle Lewis is scared to death of him, I know that.

[DOUG *begins putting food on the table.*]

LUCILLE: Oh, Lord help us. Who is the girl?

SON: I don't know.

MARY JO: Mama is to blame for him, you know. She's spoiled him—all his life. Always making him think any woman he went with wasn't good enough for him. There is nobody in my opinion that he is too good for. I told Mama the last scrape he got into with a woman, let him get out of it himself—the best way that he can.

BOB: Miss Pauline, don't you teach in high school?

PAULINE: Yes, I do, and I have some wonderful students, more like my chums than my students, I'm happy to say. Of course I can't get more than two—a sweet little black girl and a darling little white girl from Danevang—interested in poetry, but I refuse to get discouraged over that.

[LEWIS *comes in.*]

LUCILLE: Lewis, we thought you wouldn't be here for dinner.

LEWIS: I didn't think I would be able to be here, but everything has changed now. Hello, Mary Jo. Hello, girls. Hello, Bob.

MARY JO AND BOB: Hello.

SISSIE AND EMILY: Hello, Uncle Lewis.

BOB: Mary Jo, did you talk to your sister about what we were discussing on the way down here?

MARY JO: No.

[*Pause.*]

Bob has a friend . . .

BOB: Fraternity brother—I met him last week in Houston. He was there seeing some lawyer. He said he and his family were about to lose their minds worrying what the government would take in taxes when his wife's father died, and so they all got together with Father and had a good sensible talk and decided to put everything in his children's name then and there and keep the government from taking them for four hundred thousand dollars. Now, I said to Mary Jo I thought we should all get together—Lucille, Mary Jo, and Lewis and Son and me—and take a real hard look at everything, the whole picture.

LUCILLE: Son, go tell Mama Lewis is here after all. Maybe she'll change her mind and join us.

[SON *goes.*]

Let the rest of us take our seats.

[*They go into the dining room.*]

MARY JO: Any special place?

LUCILLE: No.

[*They seat themselves.*]

BOB: How are you, Doug?

DOUG: I'm pretty well.

BOB: You look well.

DOUG: Thank you. You look well yourself. How is Houston coming along?

BOB: It's still there.

DOUG: There are fools that drive in every day to Houston to go to work. I say you wouldn't catch me driving sixty miles no place just to work.

BOB: Well, maybe they can't find work here.

DOUG: Hush.

BOB: When was the last time you were in Houston?

DOUG: Oh, God knows. It was before Mr. Charlie died.

BOB: Well, Sister-in-Law, what a great meal. You've done it again.

MARY JO: Sister-in-Law? Mildred cooked all this. Lucille can't boil water.

LUCILLE: You're crazy. I'm a good cook when I want to be.

MARY JO: When did you ever want to be?

BOB: How have you been, Lewis?

[*No answer from* LEWIS.]

MARY JO: Lewis, Bob asked you a question.

LEWIS: I heard him.

[*A phone rings in another part of the house.*]

MILDRED [*calling*]: Phone call for Sissie.

[SISSIE *gets up from the table.*]

SISSIE: Excuse me.

[SISSIE *goes.*]

PAULINE: Everything certainly looks good. Sweet potatoes with marshmallows and pecans are my favorite.

LUCILLE: Pauline teaches school here.

BOB: Pass the biscuits, please.

MARY JO: Now, don't overdo, Bob.

LUCILLE: Here.

[*She passes the biscuits.*]

Butter?

BOB: Yes, ma'am, butter. How long have you been teaching here, Pauline?

PAULINE: It's my second year.

LUCILLE: She loves it here, don't you, Pauline?

PAULINE: Oh yes, indeed I do.

BOB: That's nice.

[SON *and* STELLA *enter.*]

STELLA: I have news for you all. Son and Miss Pauline are getting married.

LUCILLE: Son, why didn't you tell me?

SON: I had to ask for a raise, Mama, before I could think of marriage again, and Grandmother has just agreed to give me one, so . . .

BOB: How much will you be making now, Son?

SON: Six hundred a month.

BOB: What were you making before?

SON: Four hundred.

LUCILLE: Which was much too little.

MARY JO: And you get four hundred dollars a month, Lucille?

LUCILLE: Yes, same as you and Lewis.

MARY JO: My four hundred dollars is deducted from my share of the estate. Is yours, Lewis?

LEWIS: Yes.

MARY JO: Is yours, Lucille?

LUCILLE: No. I'm on salary.

MARY JO: So that makes a thousand dollars a month being paid to you and Son by the estate, plus room and board.

LUCILLE: Yes.

MARY JO: And we get nothing unless we have to borrow it, and we have to beg to do that.

LUCILLE: We're not on charity, you know. Son and I work for what we get.

MARY JO: I know what Son does, but what do you do?

LUCILLE: My God, Mary Jo, I can't believe you sometimes. What do I do?

MARY JO: Tell me one thing you do. You have three servants waiting on you hand and foot.

LUCILLE: Want to change places with me?

MARY JO: No, I don't.

LUCILLE: Well, then don't criticize. This house would fall apart if I weren't here to see to things.

MARY JO: My foot—

BOB: Now, come on, Mary Jo.

[MARY JO *jumps up from the table.*]

MARY JO: I'm going home.

BOB: Now, Mama—

MARY JO: Now, don't "Mama" me, Bob. I'm sick of this house and this family. Everybody in this damn family gets everything they want but me. I have to get on my knees and beg to my mama for every single cent I get. Lewis can borrow all he wants—Lucille and Son get money handed out to them right and left.

LUCILLE: No one hands out anything to me. I earn every penny I get.

MARY JO: In a pig's eye.

STELLA: What do you want, Mary Jo? Just tell me, what in the name of God you want? Do you want to borrow money?

MARY JO: No, I do not want to borrow money—I am sick of borrowing money—I want the estate divided, so that me and my precious girls can have some peace for a change. Bob is too proud to tell you this, but I'm not. He's at his wit's end. He has not sold any real estate in the city of Houston for four months. He has not earned a red cent in four months.

STELLA: Well, why didn't you say so? The estate will loan you money.

MARY JO: I don't want the estate to loan me anything. I want us to divide the estate, so I can have a little dignity in my life.

[MARY JO *exits into the kitchen.*]

STELLA: Isn't anybody going to congratulate Son and Miss Pauline on their engagement?

BOB: Congratulations, Son.

SON: Thank you.

EMILY: When do you plan on getting married?

SON: Ask my wife-to-be.

PAULINE: I want to finish out this term at school at least.

BOB: Sissie is going with a lovely fellow who is in computers. He's begging her to marry him. That's who she's on the phone with right now.

LUCILLE: Son has just had a computer system installed here. It's very complicated.

PAULINE: I read in the paper this morning that the Houston public schools are in real jeopardy—busing hasn't worked at all. One man interviewed was very upset. He said he had always been a liberal, and he had favored busing in the past, but now it had destroyed the concept of the old neighborhood school. He thought neither black or white benefited by it. He said the whites were all going to private schools, leaving only blacks and Hispanics in the public schools.

EMILY: Who cares?

PAULINE: Well, I happen to care very much about our public school system. In my opinion, it has been the backbone of our nation.

LUCILLE: Do you think busing is wrong?

PAULINE: No, I didn't say it was wrong. I just said, in its present state it doesn't seem to be working . . .

[*Pause.*]

Our whole educational system is in jeopardy, it seems to me. The Japanese are surpassing us in every way because of their educational systems.

STELLA: We have a plastic factory here now, run by Japanese.

LUCILLE: Not Japanese, Mama—Taiwanese.

BOB: I fought the Japanese when I was eighteen. Don't tell me anything about the Japanese.

PAULINE: All I know is that their educational system far surpasses ours.

BOB: In what way, little lady?

PAULINE: In terms of achievement.

BOB: How much would you say your estate's worth, Mother-in-Law?

STELLA: I don't know—ask Son.

BOB: Do you know, Son?

SON: Fluctuates. Of course, you know the basis is the land—five thousand acres.

BOB: That's easily five million right there.

SON: If you can get it. Two years ago you might have gotten it. I don't know about today.

BOB: Of course you can get it—maybe more.

SON: I don't know—land values are pretty depressed around here right now.

BOB: I could get you a thousand an acre tomorrow. I have at least five friends in Houston, maybe ten, maybe fifteen.

STELLA: I thought Houston was in a depression.

BOB: Not everybody in Houston, Mother-in-Law. There is still a lot of money in Houston, but what I am driving at, the point I wish clearly to make, is that God forbid anything happened to you, the old government would slap the highest evaluation they could get by with on your land and your other assets, which I'm sure are not inconsiderable. I don't know what the house and ten acres is worth, for instance, but I could inquire if you ever want to sell it.

STELLA: This house is never going to be sold. I'm giving it to Son, if he promises never to sell it or let his children sell it, and Doug has to live out back during his lifetime.

[MARY JO *reenters from the kitchen.*]

MARY JO: Son?

STELLA: Yes, Son. S-O-N, Son.

MARY JO: When did you decide this?

STELLA: Just now.

BOB: Now, let's don't get sidetracked, Mama. For the time being, leave the house out of it. Figure, conservatively, your tax without the house would be easily a million dollars.

STELLA: A million dollars?

BOB: Yes, ma'am.

STELLA: Oh, God Almighty.

BOB: Now, I don't know what your cash situation is.

STELLA: Well, we don't have a million dollars in all, do we, Son?

SON: No, ma'am, nowhere near that.

BOB: Exactly, so you know what you have to do?

EMILY: Daddy, can't this wait until after dinner?

STELLA: Lewis has gone asleep. Wake him up, Sissie.

EMILY: I'm Emily.

STELLA: Well, where's Sissie?

EMILY: On the telephone.

MARY JO: Lewis, wake up.

[LEWIS *opens his eyes and begins eating again.*]

BOB: Mother-in-Law, what you will have to do, or your heirs will, is sell off some of the land to pay the government the inheritance tax—so that's a million dollars you are going to have to unnecessarily give to the government, thus diminishing the estate's landholdings. There is, of course, a way to avoid all this . . .

EMILY: Excuse me.

[*She gets up.*]

MARY JO: Don't you want dessert?

EMILY: No.

MARY JO: Where are you going?

EMILY: I'm going to read my *Cosmopolitan.*

[EMILY *leaves.*]

BOB: May I continue, Mary Jo?

MARY JO: I'm sorry, Bob.

BOB: Now, the best and most sensible thing, in my opinion, is to go right away to a tax expert for advice. Now, I'm sure he will tell you the way to avoid all of this is to start each year giving a part of the estate to each of your children, so that in a given number of years you can legally give them their inheritance tax-free, or practically tax-free.

LEWIS: Sounds like a good idea to me, Bob.

LUCILLE: Have you and Brother been in cahoots over this, Mary Jo?

MARY JO: What are you talking about?

LUCILLE: He was begging Mama all morning before you came about dividing the estate. Did you and Bob put that idea in his head?

LEWIS: Nobody put any idea in my head, Sister.

LUCILLE: What will happen to Son, while this is all going on? What will happen to his job managing the estate?

MARY JO: What will happen to it when Mama dies?

LUCILLE: It's Mama's intention he'll go on managing it. At least, that's what she's always told me.

MARY JO: How is he going to do that when she dies and the estate is divided? He's certainly not going to manage my share, and I doubt if Lewis will let him manage his.

LUCILLE: Last time I talked to Mama, she didn't ever want to divide the estate, she was thinking about turning the whole thing into a trust and having Son manage it—weren't you, Mama?

STELLA: That was one plan I had—

MARY JO: Seems to me you've had one too many plans. Lewis, I think we're having our birthrights stolen right in front of our very eyes by Lucille and Son.

SON: Are you crazy, all of you? I bring my fiancée here to be introduced to you, and she must think I live with a bunch of lunatics.

LUCILLE: I will not sit here and let Bob and Mary Jo take your job away from you, after you and your father have served this family so unselfishly all these years.

SON: Let them take the job, Mama. I can always find something to do.

MARY JO: After all, he will always inherit your share of the money—

SON: I don't want her share of the money. I don't want anybody's share of the money. That's all I've heard all my life. Money, money, money—

[DOUG *enters carrying a serving dish, drops it, and it shatters, spilling the food.* SON *gets up to help along with* PAULINE.]

LEWIS: My God, Doug—what are you doing?

[*He calls.*]

Mildred. Mildred.

MILDRED [*calling back*]: What?

LEWIS: Doug dropped a dish.

[MILDRED *enters and helps pick it up.*]

DOUG: I'm going to lie down. I don't feel too good.

[SON *helps* DOUG, *who goes to sit down.*]

STELLA: Come have your dinner, Son.

SON: I'm not hungry, thank you, Grandmother. I'm giving notice. You'll have to get someone else to take over here—it's really very impractical, my staying on.

STELLA: I won't give you the house if you leave.

SON: Then you won't give me the house.

LUCILLE: You won't give him the house anyway, Mama. He's no fool. You've been giving him that house and taking it back at least six times in the last year.

[*Pause.*]

Well, sit down at least, and let Pauline finish her dinner.

[SON *comes back to the table.*]

Did you ever see a family like this, Pauline?

[PAULINE *smiles. She sits and* SON *sits.* LUCILLE *goes and sits in* STELLA's *chair.*]

BOB: Do you come from a large family, Pauline?

[SON *gets up and goes to* LUCILLE.]

PAULINE: No. Just my mother and father. My father came here from North Carolina to work in the oil fields.

BOB: Well, I hope he's not dependent on the oil fields now. He's in a terrible mess if he is.

PAULINE: No, he's retired.

BOB: Where do they live?

PAULINE: Austin.

BOB: Certainly not as depressed as Houston, but it's getting there.

[LUCILLE *is crying.*]

SON: Come on, Mother.

LUCILLE: You are just like your father. You let everyone push you around and take advantage of you. Your father dropped over dead in the heat of summer while walking around those farms. That summer he had been up every day at five and never got home until dark. He fell over in the fields from exhaustion. He slaved every day for this family— not his family even, but mine, and what thanks did he get for it. What thanks did poor Charlie get for it? An early death is all he ever got. All they did was to take advantage of your father's good nature.

SON: No one's going to take advantage of me. Sit down and finish your dinner.

[LUCILLE *goes back to her place.* SON *goes to his.*]

PAULINE: Have you gotten VCRs yet?

MARY JO: We have.

PAULINE: They are lifesavers here because we have no movie theater here now.

STELLA: What was that song you were humming this morning, Son?

SON: "Rock of Ages."

STELLA: Oh, yes. You remember, they sang that at your father's funeral, children.

LEWIS: No, they didn't.

STELLA: They certainly did.

LEWIS: They did not.

LUCILLE: I thought they did, too, Lewis.

LEWIS: Well, they didn't.

STELLA: What did they sing, then?

LEWIS: "In Heavenly Love Abiding."

STELLA: How does that go?

LEWIS: I don't remember—

STELLA: Do you remember, Son?

SON [*singing*]: "In heavenly love abiding, my heart shall know no fear . . ."

BOB, LUCILLE, PAULINE, AND MARY JO [*joining in with* SON]: And safe in God's confiding, for nothing changes here . . ."

STELLA: Ever since he was a little boy, Son has always loved hymns—you should have been a preacher, Son.

SON: Maybe that wouldn't have been a bad idea.

BOB: If you leave now, do you have any prospects for a job, Son?

SON: No. I have thought about going back to college and getting a degree and then going to law school, if I can get in.

BOB: At your age?

SON: You have to start sometime—

STELLA: Well, this is just all a lot of talk. You're going no place. You're going to put all our affairs on that computer system and I'm going to raise your salary.

MARY JO: By the way, Bob, Mama says we have borrowed three hundred thousand dollars from the estate. Do you believe that?

BOB: No.

STELLA: Well, you have.

BOB: You'll have to prove it to me.

STELLA: It's all there in black and white.

MARY JO: And she says that Lewis has borrowed two hundred thousand, and I certainly don't believe that.

LEWIS: And neither do I.

MARY JO: Why don't you believe it?

LEWIS: Because I don't think I have.

MARY JO: Well, that's not why I don't believe it. I think if we've borrowed three hundred thousand, then you have borrowed four or five.

LUCILLE: Oh, my God. I find this all so depressing. Let's change the subject, please.

[*Pause.*]

Have you selected your silver pattern yet, Pauline?

PAULINE: No. Not yet.

LUCILLE: Your china pattern?

PAULINE: No.

MARY JO: My silver and china pattern are both discontinued.

LUCILLE: So are mine.

[DOUG *gets up from his chair and goes to the dining room table.*]

DOUG: Good night, everybody.

STELLA: It's not night, Doug—we're having our dinner, and go out in the kitchen if you're feeling better and help Mildred.

DOUG: Yes'm. I was having the sweetest dream. I dreamt I was in glory and there was angels everywhere and they were singing. My God, you never heard such singing.

STELLA: That wasn't any angel, Doug, that was Son and the others singing.

DOUG: Yes'm. I was out in the field and heard Mama hollering and come running across the fields to where she was and I said, "Mama what is it—what in the name of God is it?" And she says, "The bull killed your daddy—go yonder to the next place and get help." I ran across the fields as fast as I could to another family working on the place and I says, "Come quick, the bull has killed my daddy." And then there was the funeral and they buried my daddy and Mama says, "What's to become of us now you have no daddy and I have no husband?" And then Miss Stella's daddy came and then he says to Mama, "I'm going to take you and the boy to town so you can live on our place," and we come here and Mama cooked for these good people until she went to her rest, and we lived out yonder in the back in the house I still live in from that day on.

MARY JO: What do you pay him?

STELLA: I don't know. What do we pay him, Son?

SON: Two hundred a month.

DOUG: I'm tired, Miss Stella. I am so tired.

[DOUG *lies down on the dining room floor.*]

STELLA: Doug, get up from there. Son, take him to his room.

SON: All right.

[MILDRED *comes out.*]

MILDRED: How many wants dessert? Raise your hand.

STELLA: Doug, get up off the floor. Mercy, Son, go to him.

[SON *goes to him.*]

SON: Doug. Doug.

[*He feels his forehead, he listens for his heartbeat.*]

Poor old man, he's dead.

[SON *holds him as the lights fade.*]

ACT 2

SCENE 1

[*Two days later.* LUCILLE *is in the living room.* PAULINE *and* SON *enter from outside.*]

SON: Where is everybody?

LUCILLE: Mary Jo and Bob are looking at the farms, Mama and Lewis are upstairs taking naps, Sissie and Emily are reading and listening to music. The funeral wore Mama and Lewis out, they said. I thought it was lovely, didn't you?

SON: Yes, I did.

LUCILLE; I don't know what I had expected. Something much more emotional, I suppose. I thought you spoke beautifully about Doug, Son. Didn't you, Pauline?

PAULINE: Yes, I did. I thought he was very eloquent.

LUCILLE: That is the word—eloquent.

SON: Well, I was devoted to him.

LUCILLE: We all were. It has affected Mama very much. Brother, too. Son, I know in my heart Mary Jo and Bob are going to start in again with some kind of scheme or another to get Mama to divide the estate. Bob always has some kind of harebrained scheme to get everybody rich. Why, if Mama had listened to him and the things he wanted her to invest in, we'd all be in the poorhouse. Houston this and Houston that. All his rich friends and their rich schemes. Well, I don't see how it's helped him one bit.

SON: Mama . . .

LUCILLE: I don't think the estate should be divided just because they need money. They always need money. They live way, way beyond their means.

SON: Mama . . .

LUCILLE: Now, do not be foolish and filled with false pride. You must not give up your position here. You must not abandon all you've worked for.

SON: Mama, please—this is very difficult for me. It's not that I'm not attached to the farms, Mama—I am. Very. I mean, spring and fall, summer and winter, since I was a little boy, I've gone out there part of every day.

LUCILLE: And he has, too. First with Papa, and then with his father. When his father died, Son was eighteen and just beginning college, and Mama and I tried to manage the farms ourselves, but we didn't know how, and things just went from bad to worse, and so when he was at the beginning of his junior year in college, Mama and I wrote him and asked if he would come back here and take over for the family, and he did. And his coming back saved us.

SON: Maybe it is wisdom, Mother, to work out some plan now to avoid unreasonable inheritance taxes. Some day it will have to be divided—the day Grandmother dies. Every year the income from the estate gets less and less—the taxes increase. Every year it gets more difficult to make any kind of a profit.

LUCILLE: Some farms are making profits.

SON: I don't know how. There is only one thing that can finally save us, and that is to get an oil or gas lease.

LUCILLE: Well, we never have in all these years . . .

SON: I know, and I don't really think we will now, but there is interest in land out that way now. I have been called on twice about a prospective lease.

LUCILLE: Oh, Son, wouldn't that be wonderful!

SON: Yes, I suppose it would. Wonderful and sad. Sad because it means we no longer know how to make a living out of our land unless we find oil and gas there.

LUCILLE: How much do you think an oil or gas lease would bring the estate?

SON: Oh, I don't know. That would have to be negotiated, but Mama, don't in any way get your hopes up about that. In all these years, we have never had one, and we likely won't get one now.

LUCILLE: But I hear with the new technology, they are finding oil and gas in places they never could find it before.

SON: That's true.

LUCILLE: Well, I'm certainly not going to lose any sleep worrying about it.

[*Pause.*]

But if they make an offer for an oil or gas lease, how much do you think we could expect?

SON: Enough to pay our taxes this year.

LUCILLE: Is that all?

[MARY JO *and* BOB *enter.*]

MARY JO: What's this about oil and gas?

SON: I was just telling Mother that in the last few days I had two inquiries about a lease on our land by an oil and gas company.

MARY JO: Why weren't we informed?

SON: Because there was nothing to inform you about. A scout called me twice and asked about the location of the land, and was it leased, and had it ever been leased . . .

BOB: I was talking just now uptown to Damon Jackson. He made a fortune in oil, you know—many years ago when they first—

MARY JO: I wish in the future to be informed if there is oil interest in our estate.

SON: It was only two phone calls.

MARY JO: I don't care if it is only one phone call. I want to be informed.

SON: All right, I'll inform you. I am supposed to call him back this afternoon, and if there is anything to report, I'll tell you.

LUCILLE: Son says you don't get a lot from an oil lease.

BOB: That is true. The big money starts if you strike oil!

MARY JO: How much would we get from an oil lease?

SON: Depends how bad they want the lease.

MARY JO: Well, how much?

SON: I hear lately some people are getting twenty thousand dollars for a year.

MARY JO: Twenty thousand dollars, is that all?

SON: That's all! And that's tops around here, but you have to first get a lease so they'll drill, and of course if they strike oil . . .

MARY JO: Well, how much would we get if they strike oil?

SON: Not as much now with the price of oil so low, but still plenty.

LUCILLE: Of course in the old days those that had the land over by Boling and New Gulf were the ones that really got rich. That's where they found sulfur, you know.

PAULINE: Have you heard the horrible things they are trying to do out there? Some French company has bought the sulfur company from Texas Gulf and they are trying to lease the pockets left underground when the sulfur was removed to some other French company for the storage of chemical wastes.

SON: When did you hear about this?

PAULINE: I just heard about it. Do you know what that can mean to us if it happens? If there is a leak of any kind, or an accident, the water supply of this part of the Gulf Coast could be poisoned.

LUCILLE: No.

PAULINE: It certainly could.

[LEWIS *comes in.*]

LEWIS: I thought I heard someone down here.

[*Pause.*]

Son, I want to apologize to you and Pauline for the way I've been acting. I was drunk, and I'm truly sorry.

SON: That's all right, Uncle Lewis.

LEWIS: I'm fond of you, Son.

SON: I know that, Uncle Lewis, and I'm fond of you, too.

LEWIS: And I appreciate all you have done for this family.

SON: Thank you.

LEWIS: Pauline, when his father died, I said to myself, I'll try to be the father to him that death had so cruelly taken away. As a matter of fact, that first night sitting here by Charlie's coffin, I said to Son, "Son, I'm going to make up to you, in all ways, the father you have lost." Do you remember my saying that to you, Son?

SON: Yes, I do.

LEWIS: And I wanted to, you know, but then my weakness would get the best of me, that terrible weakness that almost wrecked my life; and I apologize profusely to you.

SON: Now, now, Uncle Lewis.

LEWIS: I thought you spoke eloquently at Doug's funeral.

SON: Thank you.

LEWIS: I wanted to speak, but I was too emotional—I didn't dare try.

BOB: I called a fine tax lawyer in Houston and asked him if he could recommend a tax lawyer here that we could consult, but he said he thought we'd be wasting our time talking to a lawyer here when I told him the size of the estate.

LEWIS: What do you want a tax lawyer for?

BOB: Don't you remember our conversation at dinner the day Doug died?

LEWIS: No.

MARY JO: Oh, come on, Lewis. You weren't that drunk.

LEWIS: I don't remember it. I'm sorry.

MARY JO: You don't remember Bob explaining what could happen to the estate if Mama . . .

LUCILLE: Well, don't anyone mention death to Mama today. I warn you, she's very depressed.

MARY JO: No one wants to talk to Mama about anything. It's just that since Son said he was leaving his job here, Bob and I talked it over . . .

LUCILLE: Son is not leaving his job here.

MARY JO: Well, he said he was, right in there, unless I'm losing my mind entirely.

LUCILLE: It is certainly not definite.

LEWIS: Son, you can't leave here. Who would take care of the estate? This estate is very complicated, you know.

[SISSIE *and* EMILY *come in.*]

BOB: Why don't you girls go back and read? We're talking over some business.

EMILY: I've read until my eyes are about ready to fall out.

BOB: Watch a little television, then.

SISSIE: I don't want to.

EMILY: I don't, either.

BOB: Well, if you stay here, don't interrupt us. Like the lawyer says, "Strategy is everything."

LUCILLE: I flat-out don't want to divide the estate.

LEWIS: I don't, either.

MARY JO: You don't? Are you crazy? You were demanding we do it two days ago.

LEWIS: I was drunk. I don't want to divide the estate. And I certainly want Son to stay to see to it.

BOB: You don't have to divide anything at present. This will take a year, maybe, to work out with your Mama.

LEWIS: I don't want to divide the estate. Not now, not a year from now—

MARY JO [interrupting]: Pauline, would you mind if I give you a little advice?

PAULINE: No. Not at all.

MARY JO: Don't live on here after you and Son marry. It will drive you absolutely crazy if you do. That is what happened to his first marriage, you know. His wife, Olive Louise, said that one more meal here with this family and she would go screaming mad out of this house.

LUCILLE: Son, do you believe she said that?

SON: I don't know, Mother.

LUCILLE: Did she ever say that to you?

SON: Not in so many words.

MARY JO: She loved Son, you know. She loved him until the day she died.

LUCILLE: How do you know that?

MARY JO: Because a cousin of hers was a friend of a friend.

LUCILLE: Oh, yes—you told us that.

MARY JO: And she said she loved Son until the day she died.

LUCILLE: You've already told us that.

MARY JO: Olive Louise was always getting her cousin to call my friend to call me to see if Son was interested in any other girls. She said when she heard Son was seeing Pauline, she cried her eyes out.

LUCILLE: Oh, I don't believe that for one minute. Do you believe that, Son?

SON: How would I know, Mama?

LUCILLE: Did she ever tell you she was still in love with you?

SON: No.

BOB: Folks, let's get back on track. What I'm trying to explain to you . . .

[STELLA comes in.]

STELLA: I've been thinking all afternoon about putting Doug to rest. Oh, my—poor old fellow.

LUCILLE: Now, he had a good life, Mama.

[LEWIS *starts to cry.*]

MARY JO: Brother, what on earth is the matter?

LEWIS: I'm sorry. I'm just very emotional.

STELLA: Oh, I was thinking all afternoon of Doug and my father and my grandfather—and God knows, all kinds of things crossed my mind. I was thinking of the time you came into my room after school, Son. You asked me if we were Yankees. Why did you do that, Son? I remember your doing it, but I can't remember why.

EMILY: Are we part Yankee, Mama?

STELLA: Why did you ask me that, Son?

SON: Because Robert Daley had hollered out during history class that my grandfather was a Yankee soldier and a carpetbagger.

STELLA: It wasn't your grandfather, it was your great-great-grandfather.

SON: Whoever—and I came home very upset, and I asked you if it was true my great-grandfather was a Yankee.

STELLA: Great-great-grandfather.

EMILY: Was he, Mother?

MARY JO: Yes, he was.

SISSIE: How did he get here?

STELLA: I don't remember.

MARY JO: Oh, you do too remember, Mama.

STELLA: No, I don't.

MARY JO: Well, I certainly don't remember. What's more, I don't care.

SISSIE: Do you remember, Uncle Lewis?

LEWIS: No, I don't.

SON: I remember. At least, I remember what Grandfather told me: that Grandmother's grandfather came down here as a Union soldier during the occupation and then went back north to someplace . . .

STELLA: Illinois.

MARY JO: I thought you didn't remember.

STELLA: I remember that much.

MARY JO: You remember what you want to.

SISSIE: Well, what happened when he got back to Illinois?

SON: Well, he liked it here so much that he decided to come on back, and he was here during the Reconstruction.

STELLA: And my daddy told me that his daddy told him that you could buy land here for a dollar-fifty an acre, and people were abandoning their plantations because they couldn't make a living on them without their slaves, and he saved his money and bought as much land as he could, and that makes up our estate.

SON: That's not what that boy told me in front of the class that day. He said my great-grandfather . . .

STELLA: Great-great-grandfather.

SON: Great-great-grandfather stole everything we have. He said he was elected to a county office at the courthouse.

STELLA: County clerk.

MARY JO: You see? She remembers everything.

SON: And that he stole land right and left by destroying legal records in the courthouse.

STELLA: Which is not true, of course.

SON: And this boy said, "I bet you have a blue belly just like your Yankee great-grandfather."

STELLA: Great-great-grandfather.

SISSIE: Well, I never knew that before.

EMILY: Who did he steal the land from?

STELLA: He didn't steal the land. He didn't steal anything.

MARY JO: Well, let's change the subject. Who cares about all that? When are you going to talk to the man about—

STELLA: Son, I want you to take me for a ride in the car.

LUCILLE: Lewis can take you, Mama.

STELLA: I don't want to ride with him. His hands shake worse than Doug's. I'm afraid to ride with him.

LUCILLE: I'll take you, Mama.

STELLA: I don't want you to. I want Son to take me.

LUCILLE: Where in the world do you want to go, Mama?

STELLA: Well, I'll tell you. As I was lying in my bed thinking of Douglas, I thought, "Well, we've done everything for him we promised—a lovely funeral, a handsome coffin, a fine, big tombstone." But then I remembered that just before he died, he said he had one more thing to ask me: that after he died, to find his mama's grave and bury him next to her. He said he would take me out to the colored cemetery and

show me her grave. Well, he died before he could, and so I want to go
out there now to the colored cemetery and find her grave.

LUCILLE: What on earth for, Mama?

STELLA: To keep my promise to Doug.

LUCILLE: He's already buried, Mama. How can you possibly keep that
promise to him now?

STELLA: Well, I'll dig him up and bury him again, or dig her up and
bury her beside him.

LUCILLE: Dig her up? What will be left, Mama, after all these years? I
bet she only had a pine-board coffin.

MARY JO: Before anybody digs anybody up, Son, for God's sake, call the
man about the oil lease.

STELLA: What oil lease?

MARY JO: An oil lease on the estate. Hasn't Son told you?

STELLA: No. Not on my estate. I want no oil wells or no gas wells clut-
tering up my land. They poison the land. Ruin it forever.

MARY JO: That is so foolish, Mama.

STELLA: When my father was alive, they tried to drill for oil on our land,
and he took a shotgun and he went out there and he said, "Get off this
land of mine or I'll blow your brains out."

LEWIS: Mama, that's not true. You used to say you prayed every night we
would get an oil lease.

STELLA: Say again the eulogy you spoke at Doug's funeral.

LUCILLE: Not now, Mama.

STELLA: Yes, now. I want to hear it now. Say it, Son.

SON: All right.

[*Pause.*]

Ever since I can remember, Doug Alexander has been a great part of
my life. He was always in our house and yard when I was growing
up—never too tired or too busy to talk to me or to show me . . .

MARY JO: I think I am losing my mind. Do you mean to tell me,
Mama—

STELLA: Be quiet, Mary Jo. Son is saying Doug's eulogy.

MARY JO: I don't want to hear Doug's eulogy.

STELLA: Then leave the room.

MARY JO: I will not leave the room. I think this whole family has gone crazy. Are you going to calmly sit here and let an oil lease slip through our hands?

LEWIS: Why are you getting so excited, Mary Jo? If Mama doesn't want an oil lease, she doesn't want one. I, for one, have everything I need.

MARY JO: Well, I don't have all I need. Nor does my husband or my daughters. We are in a desperate condition—on the verge of bank-ruptcy. Do you understand? We owe money to everybody. We can lose our cars, our house . . .

STELLA: Is that true, Bob, or is that just some more of Mary Jo's tales?

BOB: I'm afraid it's true. I have to tell you good people I'm on the ropes, as they say.

MARY JO: Mama, will you please let Son call about that oil lease?

STELLA: All right. God help me, I will. If you swear to me that you will never again mention about dividing the estate.

LEWIS: I don't want to divide the estate. I am happy the way things are.

BOB: What none of you understand—

MARY JO: Be quiet, Bob.

STELLA: Son, go call that oil man about the lease.

SON: You're sure now?

STELLA: Yes, I'm sure.

[SON goes.]

I remember the eulogy I gave at Henrietta's funeral.

BOB: Who in the world is Henrietta, Mother-in-Law?

STELLA: Doug's mother.

BOB: Oh.

STELLA: I said Henrietta and her son, Doug, came to live on our place when I was a girl of six. She and her husband and her son had been tenants on one of our farms, and her husband was killed tragically by one of our bulls. I remember the day Papa brought Henrietta and her son to live in the house in our backyard. Often, after she cooked our dinner and was in her house resting, I would go and visit with her and we would talk. She was always kind and patient with me.

[Pause.]

BOB: Can we just take a second to clarify . . .

STELLA [*She gets up*]: Lewis . . .

LEWIS: Yes, Mama.

STELLA: Help me upstairs. I'm tired. I want to rest.

LEWIS: All right, Mama.

[LEWIS *helps* STELLA *up.*]

STELLA: All this talk about dividing the estate has worn me out.

LUCILLE [*as* LEWIS *and* STELLA *are leaving the room*]: Nobody has been talking about dividing the estate, Mama. We were talking about an oil lease.

[LEWIS *and* STELLA *go.*]

Well, thank God, she forgot about going out to the colored cemetery and traipsing around.

MARY JO: I'm worn out. I'm exhausted. Mama just exhausts me.

PAULINE: Hasn't it been dry? I heard last night on TV that everyone's worrying about a new dust bowl, only maybe this time it's being caused by the ozone. Do you all remember the dust bowl?

MARY JO: The what?

PAULINE: The dust bowl.

MARY JO: No.

BOB: We never had a dust bowl here, Pauline, not on the coast.

PAULINE: I'm having my class read *The Grapes of Wrath*. That's all about the dust bowl.

MARY JO: Is that so.

LUCILLE: Who wrote *The Grapes of Wrath*?

PAULINE: John Steinbeck.

LUCILLE: Oh, yes. I think I read that. What is it about?

MARY JO: Didn't you hear her? The dust bowl.

PAULINE: And the Okies.

LUCILLE: Oh, yes, I think I do remember that.

PAULINE: Remember, this family from Oklahoma are trying to get to California.

LUCILLE: Oh, yes, I have a vague memory of it.

[SON *enters.*]

MARY JO: Did you reach the oilman?

SON: Yes, he'll come tomorrow afternoon.

MARY JO: Tomorrow. I think you should see him today.

SON: He didn't want to see me today. He wants to see me tomorrow.

MARY JO: It is always tomorrow in this family. Tomorrow we'll see about the oil lease. Tomorrow . . .

[LEWIS *enters.*]

LEWIS: Son, Mama wants to see you.

[SON *leaves.*]

MARY JO: What does she want to see him about?

LEWIS: I don't know. I didn't ask her, Sister.

LUCILLE: Yes, yes, *Grapes of Wrath,* I did read that, it's a great story.

PAULINE: Yes.

MARY JO: The last book I read was . . .

[*A pause.*]

I can't remember.

BOB: *Gone with the Wind?*

MARY JO: Yes, I read that, but that wasn't the last book I read.

BOB: You can get that on videocassette now, you know. Play it on your VCR whenever you want to.

LUCILLE: *Gone with the Wind?*

BOB: Yes, ma'am.

LUCILLE: Isn't that wonderful.

PAULINE: They're talking about making a sequel to it, you know.

MARY JO: I wouldn't care for that. I think it's perfect just as it is, just perfect.

SON [*calling from offstage*]: Mama, Aunt Mary Jo, Uncle Lewis, can you come up here, please.

MARY JO: Oh, I knew it was too good to be true.

[LUCILLE, LEWIS, *and* MARY JO *leave.*]

BOB: How long have you been teaching?

PAULINE: Twelve years.

BOB: That so . . . I hope you will help me talk sense to this family about inheritance taxes and hiring a lawyer. You see, it just makes common sense. It's for everybody's benefit.

[*Pause.*]

I want to go on record as saying I think Son is mighty lucky to get you.

PAULINE: Thank you.

BOB: I mean no disrespect to the dead, but Olive Louise never fit in. Never tried to. She always had a chip on her shoulder, it seemed to me. Did you ever meet her?

PAULINE: No.

BOB: She was nice-looking but never smiled. Always seemed to have a sour expression.

[MARY JO *enters.*]

I was trying to explain to Pauline, who seems to me a very sensible girl, about my feelings about the inheritance tax, like I said . . .

[MARY JO *cries.*]

What is it, honey?

MARY JO: Mama has left us, Bob.

BOB: My God!

MARY JO: She has gone to her rest.

BOB: My God Almighty!

[*Pause.*]

Well, the estate is going to be divided now, after all these years.

[*Pause.*]

Well, she had a good full life, didn't she?

MARY JO: Yes.

BOB [*singing half to himself*]: "In heavenly love abiding . . ."

MARY JO: Yes, she had a good, full life. Son would like to see you upstairs, Pauline.

PAULINE: Thank you.

[PAULINE *goes.*]

MARY JO: Will you go call the funeral parlor, Bob? Ask them please to come get Mama?

BOB: I will. And then I'm going to call the bank and tell them we will have some money soon. I'm sure tomorrow or the next day I can borrow on our share of the estate.

MARY JO: I'm sure you can.

[BOB *starts out.*]

Bob, how much do you think our share will be?

BOB: Oh, I'd just be guessing until I see some actual figures. But enough. And it's come just in time, let me tell you.

[MARY JO *goes to him.*]

Now, now. It's going to be all right. But I was scared to death there for a while.

MARY JO: I know you were. I was, too.

BOB: I had no one to talk to. I didn't want to worry you any more than I had to; my friends were all so depressed, out of work, needing money. Well, it's going to be all right now. The estate is going to be divided. Of course, I could have saved the family thousands if they'd only listened to me.

[BOB *starts away.*]

MARY JO: Bob, just take a guess at what you think our share will be.

BOB: All right, just let me call the funeral parlor and then I'll do some figuring.

[BOB *goes.* LUCILLE *enters.*]

LUCILLE: Sister, she's at peace. Mama's at peace.

MARY JO: I know. Bless her sweet heart.

LUCILLE: Let's make a list of pallbearers.

MARY JO: All right.

LUCILLE: She said she always wanted Doug as an honorary pallbearer, but he died first.

MARY JO: Who else did she want?

LUCILLE: Son.

MARY JO: And Lewis?

LUCILLE: I asked him. He can't. He's too upset. Bob.

MARY JO: Certainly Bob.

LUCILLE: Sister, can you believe it? Mama's gone.

MARY JO: It's hard to realize.

LUCILLE: Mama's gone.

[BOB *comes in.*]

BOB: I got the funeral director. He'll be right over. He said, "Had you discussed how much you want to spend on her coffin?"

LUCILLE: I want the best. Doug had the best coffin, you know.

MARY JO: What did it cost?

LUCILLE: I don't know. You'll have to ask Son, I just knew it was the best they had.

[LEWIS *comes into the room.*]

Can you believe it, Brother? Mama's gone.

[LEWIS *begins to cry.* LUCILLE *goes to him.*]

Oh, Brother—Brother—Brother.

LEWIS: Everything will be different now.

LUCILLE: Yes, it will.

LEWIS: Everything will be different now. Everything—everything.

[*The lights fade.*]

SCENE 2

[*A week later.* EMILY, SISSIE, *and* MARY JO *are there.* MARY JO *has a piece of paper on which she is writing.*]

MARY JO: Now look around, and anything you want I'll write down and put your initial after it, and we'll ask for it. Of course, you understand you may not get it if Son or Lewis or Lucille ask for it, too. In that case, we will have to have a drawing. Mama always said that the china belonged to me and the silver to Lucille and Lewis. I hope that's in the will.

EMILY: Who gets her jewelry?

MARY JO: She said that was divided three ways, between Lucille, Lewis, and me. I have asked for the diamond brooch, but that doesn't mean I'll get it, because the minute I asked for it, Lucille said she had always wanted it. Now, let's carefully go through all the rooms and we'll write down whatever it is you'd like. We'll start in here. What would you like in here? Sissie?

SISSIE: Nothing.

MARY JO: Nothing?

SISSIE: No, ma'am. Not a single, solitary thing. In my house, I want everything new and modern.

MARY JO: Well, maybe your fiancé would like something. Did you ever think of that?

SISSIE: He wants everything new and modern, too.

MARY JO: You do not have an ounce of sentiment, do you? Not an ounce. Emily?

EMILY: Could you sell any of this?

MARY JO: Sell it? Why in the world would you want to sell what belonged to your grandmother and your great-grandmother?

EMILY: To get money.

MARY JO: Well, I don't think we're going to have to worry about money for a while now.

EMILY: How much are we going to get when the estate is divided?

MARY JO: I don't know exactly. We'll know better when Daddy and Son come back from the lawyers.

EMILY: How much do you think it will be?

MARY JO: Oh, I don't think we should speculate, girls. I really—

SISSIE: I heard you and Daddy talking last night. Daddy said he thought you might clear at least seven hundred and fifty thousand dollars if you can get them to sell this house.

MARY JO: Well, we'll soon know.

EMILY: If you get that, can I have another trip to Europe?

MARY JO: If you girls don't want anything here, what about in the dining room and the bedrooms?

SISSIE: There is not a thing in a single room in this house that I want, thank you.

EMILY: Ditto.

MARY JO: Ditto?

EMILY: Ditto.

MARY JO: What a way to talk.

EMILY: Just give me a trip to Europe and I'll be happy.

MARY JO: Well, if you don't want anything, I'm still going to pretend you do and put down things I want in your names. That way Lucille won't end up with everything. Now, I want the sofa and these chairs, and . . .

[LUCILLE enters.]

LUCILLE: Mary Jo, I went through the house early this morning and I made a list of what I would like. Have you made your list?

MARY JO: Partly.

LUCILLE: Do you want to hear mine?

MARY JO: What about Lewis? Is he making a list?

LUCILLE: No. If we live on in the house, he said just to include him in my list, as he will live on here with us. Of course, I still think if Mama left the house to Son, she certainly meant for the furnishings to stay with the house.

MARY JO: Well, we don't know that she left the house to Son, do we?

LUCILLE: Well, you heard her say in this very room she was going to.

MARY JO: I also heard her say she wasn't going to.

LUCILLE: If he quit working here, which he didn't.

MARY JO: Well, Mama said a lot of things she didn't mean. You know that as well as I do. If she put in writing somewhere she left the house to Son, that is fine with me. If she didn't, I'm not about to agree to giving him the house. Let me hear your list.

LUCILLE: All right. I'll start in this room. I would like the sofa and the two chairs. Lewis would like—

MARY JO: The sofa and the two chairs?

LUCILLE: Yes.

MARY JO: I want them, too.

LUCILLE: Well, if I know you, I'm sure you're going to want everything. You always have.

MARY JO: I want everything—what about you?

[MILDRED comes in with CATHLEEN.]

MILDRED: What you want for supper?

LUCILLE: I'll be out in a minute, Mildred.

MILDRED: Cathleen and I wants to know if you be going to keep us on here.

LUCILLE: We really are not able to make plans just yet. We'll know soon now.

CATHLEEN: Doug told me the day before he died that Miss Stella left us something in her will.

LUCILLE: She never told me that. Did she you, Mary Jo?

MARY JO: No, she didn't.

LUCILLE: But if it's in the will, you will certainly get it.

MILDRED: When will we know?

LUCILLE: Sometime this afternoon. Son and Mr. Bob are with the lawyers now.

MILDRED: Thank you.

[MILDRED *and* CATHLEEN *leave.*]

LUCILLE: Shall I continue with my list?

MARY JO: Please.

LUCILLE: I would like the two library lamps, and Lewis wants the floor lamp.

MARY JO: I want the lamps, too.

LUCILLE: You can't have everything, Mary Jo.

MARY JO: Neither can you.

[LEWIS *comes in.*]

Are you all through at the lawyers?

LEWIS: No. It all gave me a headache. I don't understand any of it, anyway.

LUCILLE: Did you look at the will?

LEWIS: Yes.

LUCILLE: Did it say she left the house to Son?

LEWIS: No.

LUCILLE: Did you tell the lawyer that she said she wanted to give the house to Son?

LEWIS: Yes. But he said that would mean nothing in a court of law unless we all agreed to give him the house. I said I agreed.

LUCILLE: And I certainly agree.

MARY JO: Well, I don't. And I don't think I'm being unreasonable. We owe the estate three hundred thousand dollars. Bob thinks this house and ten acres would bring half a million or more.

LUCILLE: And Bob is crazy.

MARY JO: Thank you, but I don't think so. Now, Bob says, and I agree, if you want to cancel our three-hundred-thousand-dollar debt, you may keep the house.

LUCILLE: What!

MARY JO: I said—

LEWIS: Be careful, Sister. Don't agree to anything without legal counsel. That is what the lawyer said. He warned the estate is a very complicated one since we have so little cash, and so much of our assets are in land. He said each of us might want to retain a lawyer. I've retained one for myself.

LUCILLE: Why?

LEWIS: To protect my interests.

LUCILLE: Oh, I think it is a shame for brothers and sisters to need lawyers.

LEWIS: It may be a shame, but you'd better get one. Bob has one.

LUCILLE: How do you know?

LEWIS: I saw him. He's over there with Bob right now, going over the will.

LUCILLE: Did you know that Bob had hired a lawyer, Mary Jo?

MARY JO: Yes, I did.

LUCILLE: My God—

[LUCILLE *leaves.*]

MARY JO: I hope, Lewis, you'll remember the girls in your will and not leave everything to Son and Lucille. I don't care about myself, but they are your nieces, you know.

LEWIS: I know, but I don't plan on dying just yet.

[LEWIS *leaves.*]

EMILY: Mama, heavens . . .

MARY JO: You have to be practical about these things, honey. If we end up with seven hundred and fifty thousand dollars, which it looks like

we will, now that the house does not belong to Son, that means that
Lewis will have that, too, and there is no reason when he dies that you
shouldn't have half of that, which will be . . .

[*Pause.*]

What is half of seven hundred and fifty thousand dollars?
EMILY: I don't know.
MARY JO: Sissie, do you know?
SISSIE: No.

[MARY JO *writes figures on her pad.*]

MARY JO: Two into seven goes three times and carry one, and two into
fifteen goes seven times and carry one, and two into ten goes five.
Three hundred and seventy-five thousand dollars. Now add that to
seven hundred and fifty thousand and you will have . . .

[*Pause.*]

just a moment. One million, one hundred twenty-five thousand
dollars.

[LUCILLE *enters.*]

LUCILLE: What is this about a million, one hundred and twenty-five
thousand dollars?
MARY JO: Nothing.
LUCILLE: Well, I hope you are not counting on anything like that from
this estate. Son says after you pay back your three hundred thousand
dollars, and the inheritance taxes are paid, and the lawyer gets his
percentage . . .
MARY JO: What percentage does the lawyer get?
LUCILLE: He told Son his fee was ten percent of the value of the estate.
MARY JO: For what?
LUCILLE: For settling the estate.
MARY JO: That's highway robbery! Get another lawyer.
LUCILLE: We can't, Son says. Mama put it in her will that he was to
settle the estate for us.
MARY JO: My God.

[LUCILLE *goes out to the kitchen.*]

I am so depressed. Lucille always paints a black picture of everything. She takes the joy out of everything. Always has.

[PAULINE *enters carrying a flowering plant.*]

Hello, Pauline. How pretty.

PAULINE: I thought you all might enjoy it.

MARY JO: Thank you. The flowers were beautiful at Mother's funeral, weren't they?

PAULINE: Yes, they were. Son not back yet?

MARY JO: No. Still with the lawyer.

PAULINE: Emily and Sissie, when Son and I marry, I would like you to be in the wedding party.

EMILY: Thank you.

MARY JO: You're having a big wedding, then?

PAULINE: I plan to. Why?

MARY JO: Nothing. It's just that I thought since Son had been married before . . .

PAULINE: I haven't been married before.

MARY JO: Of course, you haven't. You plan on marrying as soon as school is out?

PAULINE: Yes.

MARY JO: Sissie may beat you to the altar, then. She plans on marrying in early spring.

PAULINE: Will you have a big wedding, Sissie?

SISSIE: As big as we can afford. Can I have my reception at the Houston Country Club?

EMILY: You'll have to join first.

SISSIE: Well, can we join now, Mama?

MARY JO: We'll see.

SISSIE: I'd rather join the Houston Country Club than go to Europe.

EMILY: Well, I hadn't—

SISSIE: Well, you go to Europe and I'll join the Houston Country Club.

EMILY: Do you know how much that would cost to get in? Plus the yearly dues. Have you any idea?

SISSIE: Don't worry about that—let Mama and Daddy worry about that. It is Mama's money.

MARY JO: And Daddy's. What is mine is his.

[LEWIS *enters.*]

LEWIS: Not back yet?

MARY JO: No.

LEWIS: Hello, Pauline.

PAULINE: Hello.

[LUCILLE *enters.*]

LUCILLE: Well, I've hired me a lawyer, too.

LEWIS: Who did you hire?

LUCILLE: Mervin Bay.

LEWIS: I hired Ted Malone.

LUCILLE: I wouldn't trust Ted Malone as far as I could throw him, Lewis. He'll end up with everything you have.

[SON *and* BOB *enter.* LUCILLE *points to the flowers that* PAULINE *has brought in.*]

Pauline, how lovely.

MARY JO: Here they are—Bob.

LUCILLE: Well?

[*Pause.*]

SON: It's very complicated, Mama.

LUCILLE: What is?

SON: The estate. There is so little cash, you see.

LUCILLE: Well, we've known that all along.

BOB: I have a splitting headache.

MARY JO: I don't want to hear how complicated it is. Did the lawyer estimate how much we would get when it is divided?

BOB: No.

MARY JO: Why?

BOB: Well, if you'll be quiet for a minute and stop snapping questions at me, I'll try and explain. All he can do now is try to make us understand the alternatives.

MARY JO: What alternatives?

BOB: There are a couple of possible scenarios: One is a rough estimate of the value the government will put on the estate—

MARY JO: Which is?

BOB: Between five and six million, and given that figure, he made a rough estimate of what we could expect the inheritance tax to be.

MARY JO: Which is?

BOB: Well over a million dollars.

MARY JO: God Almighty.

BOB: God knows I tried to warn you all about it. Didn't I plead with you and try to get around this?

MARY JO: You certainly did, Bob.

BOB: And let me give you the bad news all at once. The lawyer figures if the estate is valued at between five and six million dollars, his fee for settling it could be between five hundred and six hundred thousand. So that's almost two million we owe already. Plus Miss Stella left a cash gift of five thousand to Mildred and five thousand to Cathleen, and twenty thousand each to two cousins out in West Texas that I never heard of.

MARY JO: You have too heard of them—Cousin Irene and Cousin Julia.

BOB: Well, if I have, I've forgotten it.

LEWIS: What is the other scenario?

BOB: The other is that since land is so devalued around here now, we can make a claim that the estate is worth about half its former value, which would make us only owe a million, if the government will accept our evaluation, which we have no assurance it will, and we could spend four or five years in appeals. No matter what, we have to raise at least a million—plus the money for the cash bequests. How much cash is there on hand now, Son?

SON: Well, we've the taxes to pay, and we have the cash for that because of the oil lease, and we have some stocks and a few bonds of about a hundred thousand that we could dispose of in a hurry, but the rest we would have to raise by selling some of the land.

MARY JO: Or this house and ten acres.

SON: Selling this house and ten acres wouldn't anywhere near cover it—it would have to be the house and some farmland.

BOB: And even if the government doesn't challenge us, it could be a year and a half before it is finally settled.

MARY JO: A year and a half?

BOB: Maybe two.

MARY JO: My God, Bob.

EMILY: You mean we won't see any of the money for two years?

BOB: Who knows if there will be any money at all? It's a terrible time now to have to sell land—unless you want to give it away. A year ago . . .

MARY JO: A year ago . . . a year ago . . . I don't want to hear about a year ago. What about now?

BOB: Nobody knows for sure about now, Mama. He says houses that were getting a hundred thousand a year ago can't find buyers at half that price. What was his estimate for this house and acreage, Son?

SON: A hundred and fifty thousand dollars, if we can find a buyer.

MARY JO: A hundred and fifty thousand dollars for this lovely old house and ten acres?

BOB: Nobody wants this big old house, Mama. If they want anything, it would be the land. They will just tear the house down.

MARY JO: It's all so depressing. What are we going to do?

BOB: What can we do?

MARY JO: Stop going around in circles. Just tell me how much will I get.

BOB: If the government insists on valuing the land at what it was once worth—say, six million, and they would get a million and a half in inheritance taxes, and the lawyer would get another six hundred thousand—that would come to over two million, and to pay those taxes and the lawyer's fee, we would have to sell land in a hurry at very low prices.

MARY JO: I don't want to hear all of that. I just want to know how much will I get.

BOB: Very little.

MARY JO: Very little. How much is very little?

BOB: After we pay off what we owe the estate, maybe a hundred thousand dollars, we could end up with as little as sixty thousand.

MARY JO: I am sick. Of course, Son and Lucille will both come out very well. You'll have three hundred thousand from us, two hundred thousand from Lewis . . .

SON: Only if we sell the house and some of the farms. So what I suggest is this: let's not divide the estate, let's keep it intact and borrow what we have to to pay off the taxes and the lawyer. We can all live here together, form a corporation, tighten our belts until we pay off the bank loan.

BOB: And like Son says, we have an oil lease now, and they can always find oil or gas out there.

MARY JO: If we're lucky, but we're not lucky.

BOB: But we could be. Look on the bright side, Mama.

MARY JO: I will never, never come back here to live.

EMILY: And I certainly won't.

SISSIE: You wouldn't catch me dead here.

MARY JO: Never, Bob. Let's go home.

[*She starts out.*]

When can we get whatever is coming to us from the estate?

SON: Not for a year at the earliest, the lawyer says.

MARY JO: Can we borrow against what we're to get in the meantime?

SON: No. It's in probate. We can't touch it without special permission from the administrator.

MARY JO: Who is the administrator?

BOB: The lawyer.

MARY JO: Well, let's ask him.

BOB: I did—he said he can't do it.

MARY JO: Why?

BOB: It's against his principles.

MARY JO: I'm going home before I lose my mind. Come on . . .

BOB: We can't go there anymore, Mama.

MARY JO: Why?

BOB: They foreclosed on our house in Houston today, Mama.

MARY JO: Bob . . .

BOB: I'm sorry, Mama, that's how it is. I didn't want to tell you before, hoping there would be a way out once we saw the will.

[*Pause.*]

MARY JO: Well, I guess we can stay here. This house belongs to me too, now.

BOB: I'll have to go into Houston and pack our clothes. Will you come with me, Mary Jo?

MARY JO: No. I never want to see that house again.

BOB: Will you girls come with me?

EMILY: Do we have to?

BOB: Yes, you have to. Somebody has to.

SISSIE: Come on, Emily. It won't kill us.

EMILY: This means we're going to have to live here.

SISSIE: We have to live someplace. When shall we go, Daddy?

BOB: As soon as we've eaten. Son, thank you.

SON: I love this land, you know. I've thought of all the times I've walked over it. In good times and bad. With my father and my grandfather. Watched the crops grow. My heart was very sad at the thought of parting with any of it.

MARY JO: How are we all going to live here together until the estate is settled without killing each other? Can you tell me that?

PAULINE: I think it can be exciting and a real challenge to us all. We can be like the Korean and Vietnamese families moving into Houston and all over the coast—they live together, they work together.

MARY JO: Well, I'm neither Korean or Taiwanese, thank you.

PAULINE: I find the way they all work together very inspiring.

MARY JO: Please, please, Pauline. You're sweet and I know you mean well, but please . . .

[MILDRED *and* CATHLEEN *enter.*]

MILDRED: Did you all read the will?

BOB: Yes. You and Cathleen are both left five thousand dollars.

MILDRED: Good God Almighty. Did you hear that, Cathleen?

CATHLEEN: Yes, I did.

MILDRED: Didn't I tell you she was going to generously remember us? I felt it.

CATHLEEN: You sure did.

MILDRED: Excuse me for asking, but when do we get our money?

SON: Not until the estate is settled.

MILDRED: When will that be?

SON: It could be a year.

MILDRED: A year?

SON: Yes—even longer.

LUCILLE: In the meantime, Mildred, you and Cathleen will have to look for work someplace else. We are going to start doing our own work.

MILDRED: You don't mean that?

LUCILLE: Yes, I do.

MILDRED: Why?

LUCILLE: So we can pay off our debts.

MILDRED: Debts? I thought the estate was left to you.

LUCILLE: I know. It is very complicated, Mildred.

CATHLEEN: The will is in probate, Miss Mildred.

MILDRED: Probate, how do you know that?

CATHLEEN: We studied it last semester.

MILDRED: Good Lord, probate, it's always something.

[MILDRED *and* CATHLEEN *go back into the kitchen.*]

MARY JO: Well . . .

[*Pause.*]

Pauline . . .

PAULINE: Yes.

MARY JO: What about the Korean and the Vietnamese that live together. Do they get along?

PAULINE: I think so. They seem to.

LUCILLE: They have to.

MARY JO: What if they don't?

LUCILLE: Then they don't, I guess.

LEWIS: Will someone tell me one thing; why doesn't that Taiwanese man put a sign on his plastic factory? Does anyone know the answer to that?

PAULINE: I do. I heard just the other day from Priscilla Knight that works at the chamber of commerce—she said she went out and asked him, and he said in Taiwan you didn't advertise because everyone knew by the look of your building what your business was.

LUCILLE: Is that so?

LEWIS: That doesn't make sense to me. His building is made of cinder blocks and shaped like a million others I have seen.

LUCILLE: Do they go to church?

LEWIS: Who?

LUCILLE: The Taiwanese.

LEWIS: I don't know.

LUCILLE: They certainly don't go to the Baptist church. Do they go to the Methodist church, Pauline?

PAULINE: I have never seen them there.

BOB: Maybe they're not Christians.

PAULINE: The Vietnamese fishermen on the coast are Catholics.

LUCILLE: Is that so?

BOB: Just like Mexicans.

LUCILLE: There are plenty of Mexican Baptists, you know.

MARY JO: Is that so? Here?

LUCILLE: I mean here.

MARY JO: Do they go to our church?

LUCILLE: No, they go to their own church.

MARY JO: Do they preach in Mexican or English?

LUCILLE: I don't know. I've never been.

PAULINE: How do you feel about bilingual education?

MARY JO: What's that?

PAULINE: It means having two languages in the school system.

MARY JO: Two what kind of languages?

PAULINE: Well, here in Texas, because of the large Spanish-speaking population, it would mean Spanish and English.

MARY JO: I think it is absolutely insane. If you are in America, you learn American—period. What do you think about it?

PAULINE: I haven't made up my mind. There are pros and cons, like there are about everything.

LUCILLE: Maybe we should make out a schedule.

MARY JO: For what?

LUCILLE: For when Mildred and Cathleen leave.

MARY JO: When will they leave?

LUCILLE: As soon as they find other jobs. We just can't turn them out.

MARY JO: No.

LUCILLE: I thought one week you would cook and I would clean house, and the next week, I'd cook and you'd clean.

[LEWIS *gets up*.]

LEWIS: I'm going out to the cemetery and say good-night to Mama.

[*He goes.*]

MARY JO: Son, what was the name of the girl whose father Lewis gave the ten thousand dollars to?

SON: I don't know.

MARY JO: Did you ask him her name?

SON: Yes, but he wouldn't tell me.

BOB: I know her name—Vaughn Evans told me uptown today: Irene Ratliff. And to tell you the truth, Vaughn thinks he's still seeing her. I don't think he's going out to the graveyard to say good-night to anyone—I think he's going out to see her. She works just down the street at that hamburger place.

LUCILLE: McDonalds?

BOB: No, the other one.

LUCILLE: Sonic?

BOB: No. No. The other one.

LUCILLE: Whataburger?

BOB: That's right.

MARY JO: Oh, my God. The next thing is he'll be marrying her and bringing her here to live. Then there will be nine of us when Pauline moves in.

PAULINE: Let's try to look on the bright side.

MARY JO: What's the bright side?

PAULINE: I know Irene Ratliff. I taught her in high school. She is very nice.

MARY JO: Is that the bright side?

PAULINE: Yes.

MARY JO: God help us all, then. God help us all.

[*Pause.*]

I know what I'm praying for, every night down on my knees—that we strike oil. If we strike oil, then can we divide the estate?

SON: I suppose so, if everyone wants to.

MARY JO: I want to go on record right now as saying I want to. Every night on bended knees. I'm not good at this communal living. I'm not Vietnamese and I'm not Korean.

LUCILLE: I thought the girl's father said he was going to kill Lewis if he
    didn't stay away from her?

SON: That's what Uncle Lewis told me. He had to give him ten thousand
    dollars to keep him from killing him.

BOB: That's before your Grandmama died. Now the father thinks he's
    going to be rich and he's welcoming him.

MARY JO: How do you know that?

BOB: Vaughn Evans told me. He said she and her father and her mother
    came to your mama's funeral.

LUCILLE: Oh, my God.

MARY JO: Did you see them at the funeral, Lucille?

LUCILLE: No.

PAULINE: I did. She waved at me.

LUCILLE: Who did?

PAULINE: Irene Ratliff.

LUCILLE: Oh, my God.

[*Pause.*]

Of all things. Do you know what I was just thinking of just now?
The night Papa died. It was a cold December night. Bitter cold. The
day before it was warm, so warm we were almost prostrated with the
heat. Then early the next morning this fierce blue norther blew up
and we were freezing. We had fires in every fireplace in the house.
Papa wouldn't let anybody near him but Dr. Dailey, you remember,
and when we saw he was sinking fast, Brother went over to get Dr.
Dailey, but the doctor was drunk and couldn't be roused, and by the
time Brother came back, Papa was dead.

EMILY: When did he die?

LUCILLE: Let's see—nineteen sixty—is it possible?

[*Pause.*]

Papa's dead, Doug is dead, Mama, Charlie—

[*Pause.*]

Who will be next?

MARY JO: Good Lord, Lucille.

[*Pause.*]

Who were Papa's pallbearers?

LUCILLE: Mr. Scott Jordan, Elmo Douglas.

MARY JO: Mr. Leslie Crockett.

LUCILLE: Yes. All of them are dead now.

MARY JO: All of them?

LUCILLE: Every last one of them.

MARY JO: Mr. Leslie Crockett?

LUCILLE: Oh, yes. He's been dead a number of years. At least five, isn't it, Son?

SON: I think so.

MARY JO: Brother, of course, was always Mama's favorite, but I always felt I was Papa's.

LUCILLE: I didn't think so at all. I thought I was Papa's favorite.

[SISSIE *begins to cry.*]

EMILY: What's the matter with you?

SISSIE: What kind of wedding can I have now if we're so poor?

[BOB *goes to her.*]

BOB: Come on, honey.

SISSIE: Couldn't we just borrow money for the wedding, Daddy?

BOB: I don't see how if we follow Son's plan—if we borrow money from the bank for our taxes, we can take nothing from the estate again until the bank is paid off. Isn't that right, Son?

SON: Yes. I won't be able to have my salary any longer. I will have to get me another job now.

LUCILLE: Then who is going to keep the accounts and see to the farms?

SON: I'll have to do that in my spare time, Mama.

BOB: I can help him.

SON: And Uncle Lewis can no longer expect his four hundred dollars each month, or you, Mama, or you, Aunt Mary Jo.

MARY JO: What will we do?

SON: You'll have to try and get jobs, too, until the bank loan is paid off.

MARY JO: Get a job? Are you crazy? I've never worked a day in my life.

BOB: You're not going to have to work, Mary Jo. I'll get a job.

MARY JO: Where?

BOB: Here.

MARY JO: Doin' what?

BOB: Somethin'. There's bound to be a job somewhere. The girls can get jobs.

EMILY: Doin' what?

BOB: I don't know. Somethin'.

MARY JO: And you expect Lewis to get a job?

BOB: He'll have to.

[*Pause.*]

MARY JO: My God. It has all changed. Hasn't it? So quickly.

[*Pause.*]

When will they start drilling on our land, Son?

SON: An oil company will never tell you that. Maybe tomorrow, maybe next week, maybe next month. The lease says they have a year.

LUCILLE: I can get a job, I suppose, if I have to.

MARY JO: What can you do? You've never worked a day in your life.

LUCILLE: Well, Grace Ann Davis had never worked a day in her life either, but when Mr. Davis died and left no money and she was penniless, she went to Austin and got a job working in a cafeteria.

MARY JO: Well, there's no cafeteria here. Maybe we could get a job at Whataburger with Brother's girlfriend. I can just see the four of us: Lucille, Sissie, Emily, and me all working at Whataburger with Brother's girlfriend.

SISSIE: Don't be funny, Mama.

PAULINE: That's what they say America is becoming, you know, a service economy.

LUCILLE: Who says it?

PAULINE: I'm always reading it somewhere—*Time* or *Newsweek*. One or the other is always saying it.

[LEWIS *and* IRENE RATLIFF *come in.*]

LEWIS: Folks, I want you to meet a dear friend of mine, Irene Ratliff.

PAULINE: Hello, Irene.

IRENE: Hello, Miss Pauline.

LEWIS: This is my sister Lucille, my sister Mary Jo, my nephew Son.

IRENE: Howdy.

OTHERS: Hello.

LEWIS: Irene works at the Whataburger. I stopped off to get a bite to eat and she was just finishing work, so I asked her to come over here with me to meet you all.

IRENE: I am so sorry about your mother. I went to the funeral with my mama and daddy. I thought it was a very nice funeral. A big crowd, too. My daddy said there are not many people in this town could fill a church like she done. Did anybody count how many came?

LUCILLE: No, I don't believe we have.

IRENE: My daddy said if he was guessing, he'd guess near two hundred. Mama said she thought nearer three hundred, and my daddy said, "Of course you'd say that, you exaggerate everything," and Mama got mad at him then—the least thing he says can get her mad—and she said, "You'll be lucky if we can get five people to come to your funeral, mean as you are."

MARY JO: Every night I'm going to pray. On bended knee—pray.

IRENE: What are you praying for, Mrs. . . . ?

MARY JO: That we strike oil, so we can divide the estate.

IRENE: Oh. My mama told me that her mama told her that her grand-daddy struck oil out on his farm a long time ago. He couldn't read or write, and he went crazy with all the money from oil and had a lot of kids, twelve, I think. And he went down and bought them all cars— big expensive cars, REOs and Packards and Buicks—and they moved into town here from the country and parked all the cars out under the chinaberry trees, and everybody in town used to ride by their house to see all them new cars parked in the yard, and one day a man from the valley came to town and knew my great-granddaddy couldn't read or write and he took advantage of him and sold him some land . . .

MARY JO: On bended knees. On bended knees.

LUCILLE: What happened to the land?

IRENE: Well, Mama says when her granddaddy went out to the valley to look at the land he bought, it was all underwater and worthless. And all that was left to show for all of his oil money was them cars he bought his kids. She said people in town used to ride by all the time to see all them cars sitting under the chinaberry trees.

LUCILLE: Under the chinaberry trees. My.

LEWIS: You remember Irene's grandfather. He ended up as the town night watchman. John Moon.

LUCILLE: Oh, yes.

LEWIS: We had this joke—John Moon only comes out at night.

MARY JO: I'm praying every night on bended knees.

IRENE: Ma'am.

MARY JO: Praying every night for my deliverance on bended knees. Praying we strike oil.

IRENE: Yes, ma'am.

LUCILLE: John Moon. Yes, I remember him.

IRENE: All I say is, if you strike oil, watch out for crooks from the valley. They will sell you land underwater every time. Every time.

LUCILLE: John Moon. My, I hadn't thought about him for the longest kind of time.

MARY JO: I'm praying . . . I'm praying . . .

[*Curtain.*]

THE TRIP TO BOUNTIFUL

A NOTE FROM THE DIRECTOR

The director tells the designer, "The sets should float on and off magically—no stagehands visible. We want to keep Mrs. Watts in view between the Houston apartment and the Houston bus station, between the Harrison bus station and Bountiful. The playwright has requested the play be done without intermission."

Designs are presented to accommodate these decisions. Why the decisions are made is often discovered only later, upon reflection. As rehearsal progressed, the reasons for decisions made instinctually became clear: the movement of the sets and the lack of intermission were creating a feeling of constant movement, an uninterrupted journey, an inevitable odyssey. Mrs. Watts steps from the quotidian reality of the Houston apartment directly into the bus station. The bus set floats onstage out of the blackness, stars framing the scene. The Harrison bus station moves onstage, the agent asleep in his cubicle. The chivalrous Sheriff helps Mrs. Watts to her feet as the Harrison station disappears and Bountiful is revealed.

The play, one was discovering, had something out of a dream about it—something mythic too: the Traveler meets archetypical figures on the way to his or her destiny. That would be simplistic and reductive as a description of the play, but it is a significant element within it. And the set changes seem to be very much in keeping.

The journey of *The Trip to Bountiful* ran about one hundred and five minutes. Although the playwright (and the director) prefer the play to be done without an intermission, should subsequent producers feel the need for a break, Mr. Foote (and the director) would have it placed after the Houston bus station and before the bus scene (between scene 3 and scene 4).

—Harris Yulin

PRODUCTION HISTORY

The Trip to Bountiful was presented by Signature Theatre Company (Kate M. Lipuma, executive director; James Houghton, founding artistic director; Beth Whitaker, artistic associate) at Peter Norton Space in New York City on December 4, 2005. It was directed by Harris Yulin, with set design by E. David Cosier, costume design by Martin Pakledinaz, and lighting design by John McKernon. Cole Bonenberger was the production stage manager, and Winnie Y. Lok was the assistant stage manager.

Carrie Watts	Lois Smith
Ludie Watts	Devon Abner
Jessie Mae Watts	Hallie Foote
Thelma	Meghan Andrews
First Ticket Agent (Houston)	Gene Jones
Second Ticket Agent (Houston)	Sam Kitchin
Roy (Harrison Ticket Agent)	Frank Girardeau
Sheriff	James DeMarse

CHARACTERS

Carrie Watts
Ludie Watts
Jessie Mae Watts
Thelma
First Ticket Agent (Houston)
Second Ticket Agent (Houston)
Roy (Harrison Ticket Agent)
Sheriff

SCENE 1

[1953, Houston, Texas. The lights are slowly brought up, and we see the living room and bedroom of a small apartment. The two rooms have been furnished on very little money. The living room is downstage right. Upstage of the room is a door leading out to the hallway. At the other end of this hallway is a door leading to the bedroom, which is downstage right. To get back and forth, then, between these two rooms, it is necessary to go out into the hallway. Upstage right is an unseen door leading to the outside stairs. Upstage left from the hallway are the unseen kitchen and bathroom.

In the living room is a daybed that has been made up for the night. Center right, in the living room, is a window looking out on the street. Stage right is a wardrobe in which MRS. WATTS'S *clothes and other belongings are kept. On top of the wardrobe are a suitcase and* MRS. WATTS'S *purse. A rocking chair is beside the window, and in the center of the room is a table with two chairs. Against the rear wall, stage left of the door, is a desk, and on the desk are a phone, a book, a newspaper, a radio, and a movie magazine.*

A full moon shines in the window. The two rooms are kept immaculately.

The bedroom is smaller than the living room. There is a bed with its headboard against the stage left wall. A small table stands by the bed. Right center is a chair for a vanity, and a dresser stands against the upstage wall, stage left of the door. Upstage left is a closet with dresses hanging in it.

In the living room MRS. CARRIE WATTS *is sitting in the rocking chair, rocking back and forth. She lives in the apartment with her son,* LUDIE, *and her daughter-in-law,* JESSIE MAE.

The lights are out in the bedroom, and we can't see much. JESSIE MAE *is asleep in bed.* LUDIE *sits on the edge of the bed. He slips out of the room.*

MRS. WATTS *continues to rock back and forth in the chair. She doesn't hear* LUDIE. *She hums a hymn to herself,* "There's Not a Friend Like the Lowly Jesus." *Then she hears* LUDIE.

LUDIE *has on pajamas and a robe.* LUDIE *has had a difficult life. He had been employed as an accountant until his health broke down. He was unable to work for two years. His mother and his wife are both dependent on him, and their small savings were depleted during his illness. Now he has started working again but at a very small salary.*

LUDIE *sneaks into the living room and picks up a book from the desk. He is about to sneak out.*]

MRS. WATTS: Don't be afraid of makin' noise, Sonny. I'm awake.
LUDIE: Yes, ma'am.
MRS. WATTS: Pretty night.
LUDIE: Sure is.
MRS. WATTS: Couldn't you sleep?
LUDIE: No, ma'am.
MRS. WATTS: Why couldn't you sleep?
LUDIE: I just couldn't.

[MRS. WATTS *turns away from* LUDIE *to look out the window again. She resumes her rocking and humming to herself. She opens and closes her hands nervously.*]

Couldn't you sleep?
MRS. WATTS: No. I haven't been to bed at all.

[*From the street beyond the front window comes the sound of a car's brakes grinding to a sudden stop.*]

LUDIE: There's going to be a bad accident at that corner one of these days.
MRS. WATTS: I wouldn't be surprised. I think the whole state of Texas is going to meet its death on the highways.

[*Pause.*]

I don't see what pleasure they get drivin' these cars as fast as they do. Do you?
LUDIE: No, ma'am.

[*Pause.* MRS. WATTS *goes back to her humming and her rocking.*]

But there's a lot of things I don't understand. Never did and never will, I guess.

[*Pause.*]

MRS. WATTS: Is Jessie Mae asleep?

LUDIE: Yes, ma'am. That's why I thought I'd better come out here. I got to tossin' an' turnin' so I was afraid I was gonna wake up Jessie Mae.

[*Pause.*]

MRS. WATTS: You're not worryin' about your job, are you, Sonny?

LUDIE [*taking a chair from the table and sitting next to his mother*]: No, ma'am. I don't think so. Everybody seems to like me there. I'm thinking about askin' for a raise.

MRS. WATTS: You should, hard as you work.

LUDIE: Why couldn't you sleep, Mama?

MRS. WATTS: Because there's a full moon. [*She rocks back and forth, opening and closing her hands.*] I never could sleep when there was a full moon. Even back in Bountiful when I'd been working out in the fields all day, and I'd be so tired I'd think my legs would give out on me, let there be a full moon and I'd just toss the night through. I've given up trying to sleep on nights like this. I just sit and watch out the window and think my thoughts. I used to love to look out the window back at Bountiful. Once when you were little and there was a full moon, I woke you up and dressed you and took you for a walk with me. Do you remember?

LUDIE: No, ma'am.

MRS. WATTS: You don't?

LUDIE: No, ma'am.

MRS. WATTS: I do. I remember just like it was yesterday. I dressed you and took you outside and there was an old dog howlin' away off somewhere and you got scared an' started cryin' an' I said, "Son, why are you cryin'?" You said someone had told you that when a dog howled a person was dyin' some place. I held you close to me, because you were tremblin' with fear. An' then you asked me to explain to you about dyin', an' I said you were too young to worry about things like that for a long time to come.

[*Pause. She looks at* LUDIE. *She sees he is lost in his own thoughts.*]

A penny for your thoughts.

LUDIE: Ma'am?

MRS. WATTS: A penny for your thoughts.

LUDIE: I didn't have any, Mama.

[MRS. WATTS *goes back to her rocking.*]

I wish we had a yard here. Part of my trouble is that I get no exercise.

[*Pause.*]

Funny the things you think about when you can't sleep. I was trying to think of the song I used to like to hear you sing back home. I'd always laugh when you'd sing it.

MRS. WATTS: Which song was that, son?

LUDIE: I don't remember the name. I just remember I'd always laugh when you'd sing it.

[*Pause.* MRS. WATTS *thinks a moment.*]

MRS. WATTS: Oh, yes. That old song.

[*She thinks for another moment.*]

What was the name of it?

LUDIE: I don't know.

[*Pause.*]

MRS. WATTS: Let's see. Oh, I hate not to be able to think of something. It's on the tip of my tongue.

[*Pause. She thinks. She sings the song.*]

Hush little baby, don't say a word.
Mama's gonna buy you a mockin' bird.
And if that mockin' bird don't sing,
Mama's gonna buy you a diamond ring.

I used to think I was gonna buy you the world back in those days. I remember remarking that to my Papa. He said the world can't be bought. I didn't rightly understand what he meant then.

[*She suddenly turns to him, taking his hand.*]

Ludie.

[*He looks at her, almost afraid of the question she intends to ask. She sees his fear and decides not to ask it. She lets go of his hand.*]

Nothin'. Nothin'.

[*Pause.*]

Would you like me to get you some hot milk?

LUDIE: Yes, ma'am. If you don't mind.

MRS. WATTS: I don't mind at all.

[*She gets up out of her chair and starts to exit to the kitchen. She begins to sing.*]

Hush little baby, don't say a word.
Mama's gonna buy you a mockin' bird.
And if that mockin' bird don't sing,
Mama's gonna buy you a diamond ring.

[JESSIE MAE, *in the bedroom, wakes up. She gets out of bed and puts on a dressing gown.*]

JESSIE MAE [*from the bedroom*]: Ludie! Ludie!

LUDIE: Come in, Jessie Mae. Mama's not asleep.

MRS. WATTS: You want butter and pepper and salt in it?

LUDIE: Yes, ma'am, if it's not too much trouble.

MRS. WATTS: No trouble at all.

[*She exits to the kitchen via the hallway.*]

[JESSIE MAE *puts on a bathrobe, then comes out of the bedroom through the hallway into the living room. She immediately turns on the lights.*]

JESSIE MAE: Why don't you turn on the lights? What's the sense of sitting around in the dark? I don't know what woke me up. I was sleeping as sound as a log. All of a sudden I woke up and looked over in bed and you weren't there. Where is your mama?

LUDIE: In the kitchen.

JESSIE MAE: What's she doing out there?

LUDIE: Fixing some hot milk for me.

JESSIE MAE [*glancing out the hallway*]: Putter, putter, putter. Honestly! Couldn't you sleep?

LUDIE: Uh-uh.

JESSIE MAE: How do you expect to work tomorrow if you don't get your sleep, Ludie?

LUDIE: I'm hopin' the hot milk will make me sleepy. I slept last night. I
  don't know what got into me tonight.
JESSIE MAE: You didn't sleep the night before last.
LUDIE: I know. But I slept the night before that.
JESSIE MAE: I don't think your mama has even been to bed.

[MRS. WATTS *comes in from the hallway with the milk.*]

  What's the matter with you that you can't sleep, Mother Watts?
MRS. WATTS: It's a full moon, Jessie Mae.
JESSIE MAE: What's that got to do with it?
MRS. WATTS: I never could sleep when there's a full moon.
JESSIE MAE: That's just your imagination.

[MRS. WATTS *doesn't answer. She hands* LUDIE *the hot milk.*]

  I don't know what's the matter with you all. I never had trouble sleepin'
  in my life. I guess I have a clear conscience.

[JESSIE MAE *picks up a movie magazine from the desk.*]

  The only time that I remember having had any trouble sleeping
  was the night I spent out at Bountiful. The mosquitoes like to have
  chewed me up. I never saw such mosquitoes. Regular gallow nippers.
  Mother Watts, where did you put that recipe that Rosella gave me on
  the phone today?
MRS. WATTS: What recipe was that, Jessie Mae?
JESSIE MAE: What recipe was that? She only gave me one. The one I
  wrote down while I was talkin' to Rosella this mornin'. You remem-
  ber, I asked you to find me a pencil.
MRS. WATTS: Yes, I remember something about it.
JESSIE MAE: Then I handed it to you and asked you to put it away on the
  top of my dresser.
MRS. WATTS: Jessie Mae, I don't remember you havin' given me any
  recipe.
JESSIE MAE: Well, I did.
MRS. WATTS: I certainly have no recollection of it.
JESSIE MAE: You don't?
MRS. WATTS: No, ma'am.

JESSIE MAE: I swear, Mother Watts, you just don't have any memory at all anymore.

MRS. WATTS: Jessie Mae, I think I—

JESSIE MAE: I gave it to you this mornin' in this very room and I said to please put it on my dresser and you said I will and went holding it in your hand.

MRS. WATTS: I did?

JESSIE MAE: Yes, you did.

MRS. WATTS: Did you look on your dresser?

JESSIE MAE: Yes, ma'am.

MRS. WATTS: And it wasn't there?

JESSIE MAE: No, ma'am. I looked just before I went to bed.

MRS. WATTS: Oh. Well, let me look around.

[MRS. WATTS *gets up and goes out the door into the hallway.*]

JESSIE MAE: I swear. Have you noticed how forgetful she is getting?

[JESSIE MAE *goes over to a small radio on the desk and turns it on. The radio plays a tune.*]

I think her memory is definitely going. Honestly, it just gets on my nerves. We're just gonna have to get out a little more, Ludie. No wonder you can't sleep. You get up in the morning, you go to work, you come home, you have your supper, read the paper, and then go right off to bed. Every couple I know goes out three to four times a week. I know we couldn't afford it before, so I kept quiet about it. But now you are working again I don't think a picture show once or twice a week would break us. We don't have a car. We don't go to nightclubs. We have to do something.

LUDIE: OK. Why don't we go out one night this week?

JESSIE MAE: I mean, I think we have to. I was talkin' to Rosella about it this morning on the phone and she said she just didn't see how we stood it. Well, I said, Rosella, we have Mother Watts and it's hard for us to leave her alone.

LUDIE: When did you and Rosella get friendly again?

JESSIE MAE: This morning. She just all of a sudden called me up on the telephone. She said she would quit being mad if I would. I said shucks, I wasn't mad in the first place. She was the one that was mad.

I told her I was plain-spoken and said exactly what I felt and people will just have to take me as I am or leave me alone. I said furthermore, I had told her the truth when I remarked that the beauty parlor must have seen her coming a long way down the road when they charged her good money for that last permanent they gave her. She said she agreed with me now entirely and had stopped patronizing that beauty shop.

[*Pause.*]

Rosella found out definitely that she can't have any children . . .

[MRS. WATTS *comes into the living room.*]

[*To* MRS. WATTS] Walk, don't run.

[MRS. WATTS *looks around the room for the recipe. Pause.*]

[*To* LUDIE] You know your mother's pension check didn't come today. It's the eighteenth. I swear it was due. I just can't understand the government. Always late.
[*To* MRS. WATTS] Did you find it?
MRS. WATTS: Not yet.
JESSIE MAE: Well, then forget about it. Look for it in the morning.
MRS. WATTS: No, I am going to look for it until I find it.

[MRS. WATTS *goes out of the room.*]

JESSIE MAE: Honestly, Ludie, she's so stubborn.

[*The radio is playing Johnny Ray's version of "Cry" or something similar.*]

I just love this song and this singer. I could just listen to him all day.

[JESSIE MAE *turns up the radio and begins to sing along. There is an immediate knocking upstairs. She is very angry.*]

Now what are they knocking about? Do you consider this on too loud?
LUDIE: No sense in arguing with them, Jessie Mae.
JESSIE MAE: They'd like it if we didn't breathe.
LUDIE: Well, it is kinda late.

[LUDIE *turns the radio off, then goes to the rocking chair and sits.*]

JESSIE MAE: Who played the captain in *Mutiny on the Bounty?*
LUDIE: Search me.
JESSIE MAE: They are running a contest in here but I never saw such hard questions.

[*Pause. She gets a chair, puts it next to* LUDIE, *and sits.*]

Rosella said Jim used to have trouble sleepin'. She said a man told him to lie in bed and count backwards and that would cure him. He tried it and she said it did. She said you start with a hundred and instead of going forward you go backwards. One hundred, ninety-nine, ninety-eight, ninety-seven, ninety-six, ninety-five . . . She said it would just knock him out.

LUDIE: Jessie Mae, maybe we can take in a baseball game one night this week. The series is getting exciting. I think Houston has the best team they've had in a long time. I'd sure like to be there when they play Shreveport.

[*Pause.*]

I used to play baseball back at Bountiful. I used to rather play baseball than eat, when I was a kid.

JESSIE MAE: Come on, let's go to bed.

[*She gets up. There is another screech of brakes.*]

There goes another car smashed up.

[*She stands behind* LUDIE, *who is still in the rocking chair.*]

Nope, they missed each other. Six cars smashed up on the freeway to Galveston, I read yesterday in the *Chronicle*. One right on top of another. I bet they were all drunk. Been down to Galveston. Gamblin', likely. I think the whole of Houston goes to Galveston gambling and drinking. Everybody but us. I don't see how some people hold down a job the ways they drink and gamble. Do you?

[LUDIE *gets up from the rocking chair and replaces the chair* JESSIE MAE *used.* JESSIE MAE *takes her magazine from the table and brings it back to the desk.*]

LUDIE: No . . . I don't.

JESSIE MAE: That's why I told Rosella I could hardly keep from callin' up your boss and givin' him a piece of my mind for payin' you the salary he pays you. Like I said to Rosella, you're so steady and so conscientious and they just take advantage of your good nature. Maybe you're too steady, Ludie.

[*Pause.* MRS. WATTS *goes into the bedroom and begins a systematic search for the recipe.*]

[*To* LUDIE] Rosella was glad to hear you're workin' again. She said she was cleanin' out some drawers night before last and had come across some pictures of you and me she'd taken when we started goin' together. I said I don't care to see them. No, thank you.

[MRS. WATTS *is looking, now, in* JESSIE MAE's *dresser drawer. She finds the recipe.*]

The passin' of time makes me sad. That's why I never want a house with the room to keep a lot of junk in to remind you of things you're better off forgetting. If we ever get any money, you wouldn't catch me buying a house. I'd move into a hotel and have me room service.

[MRS. WATTS *comes into the living room, holding the recipe.*]

MRS. WATTS: Here's your recipe, Jessie Mae.

JESSIE MAE: Thank you, but I told you not to bother. Where did you find it?

[JESSIE MAE *takes the recipe.*]

MRS. WATTS: In your room.

JESSIE MAE: In my room?

MRS. WATTS: Yes, ma'am.

[*She sits in the rocking chair.*]

JESSIE MAE: Where in my room?

MRS. WATTS: In your dresser drawer. Left-hand side.

JESSIE MAE: In my dresser drawer?

MRS. WATTS: Yes, ma'am. I looked on top of the dresser and it wasn't there an' something said to me . . .

JESSIE MAE: Mother Watts.

MRS. WATTS: Ma'am.

JESSIE MAE: Ludie, how many times have I asked her never to go into my dresser drawer?

MRS. WATTS: I thought you wanted me to find your recipe?

JESSIE MAE: Well, I don't want you to go into my dresser drawers. I'd like a little privacy if you don't mind.

MRS. WATTS: Yes, ma'am.

JESSIE MAE: And just let me never catch you looking in them again. For anything. I can't stand people snoopin' in my dresser drawers.

[MRS. WATTS *grabs the paper from* JESSIE MAE *and throws it on the floor. She is hurt and angry.*]

MRS. WATTS: All right. Then the next time you find it yourself.

JESSIE MAE: Pick that recipe up, if you please.

MRS. WATTS: Pick it up yourself. I have no intention of picking it up.

JESSIE MAE [*shouting*]: You pick that up!

MRS. WATTS [*shouting back*]: I won't.

LUDIE: Mama.

JESSIE MAE [*shouting even louder*]: You will!

LUDIE: Jessie Mae. For God sakes! You're both acting like children. It's one-thirty in the morning.

JESSIE MAE: You tell her to pick that up.

MRS. WATTS: I won't.

JESSIE MAE [*screaming*]: You will! This is my house and you'll do as you're told.

[LUDIE *walks out of the room. He goes into his bedroom.* JESSIE MAE *crosses to* MRS. WATTS.]

Now, I hope you're satisfied. You've got Ludie good and upset. He won't sleep for the rest of the night. What do you want to do? Get him sick again?

[*There is a knocking upstairs.* JESSIE MAE *screams up at them.*]

Shut up.
[*To* MRS. WATTS] You're going to go too far with me one of these days, old lady.

[JESSIE MAE *walks out of the room.* MRS. WATTS *is ready to scream back at her, but she controls the impulse. She takes her anger out in rocking violently back and forth.* JESSIE MAE *throws open the door to the bedroom and comes in.* LUDIE *is sitting on the edge of the bed.* JESSIE MAE *marches over to the vanity and sits.*]

I just can't stand this, Ludie. I'm at the end of my rope. I won't take being insulted by your mother or anyone else. You hear that?

[LUDIE *rises and stands uncomfortably for a moment. He turns and goes out the bedroom door and into the living room. He stands by the living room door, looking at his mother. She stops her rocking. He picks up the recipe.*]

LUDIE: Mama. Will you give this recipe to Jessie Mae?
MRS. WATTS: All right, Ludie.

[MRS. WATTS *takes the recipe. She starts out of the living room and* LUDIE *stops her. He obviously hates asking the next question.*]

LUDIE: Mama, will you please tell Jessie Mae you're sorry?
MRS. WATTS: Ludie . . .
LUDIE: Please, Mama.
MRS. WATTS: All right, Ludie.
LUDIE: Jessie Mae.

[MRS. WATTS *goes out of the room to the bedroom.*]

JESSIE MAE: What do you want, Ludie?
LUDIE: Mama has something to say to you.
JESSIE MAE: What is it?

[MRS. WATTS *hands her the recipe.* LUDIE *watches from the bedroom door.*]

MRS. WATTS: I'm sorry, Jessie Mae, for throwing the recipe on the floor.
JESSIE MAE: I accept your apology.
  [MRS. WATTS *goes out and reappears in the living room. Calling:*] Come on, Ludie. Let's all go to bed.
LUDIE: All right.

[*He starts for the living room door.*]

JESSIE MAE [*calling*]: And you'd better go to bed too, Mother Watts. A woman your age ought to have better sense than to sit up half the night.

MRS. WATTS: Yes, ma'am.

LUDIE: Good night, Mama.

MRS. WATTS: Good night, Ludie.

[LUDIE *waits until his mother sits in the rocking chair, and then he turns the lights off in the living room and goes into the bedroom, taking his book with him.* MRS. WATTS *buries her face in her hands. She is crying.*]

LUDIE [*now in bedroom*]: Jessie Mae. I know it's hard and all, but for your own sake, I just think sometimes if you'd try to ignore certain things.

JESSIE MAE: Ignore? How can you ignore something when it's done right under your very nose?

LUDIE: Look, Jessie Mae.

JESSIE MAE: I know her, Ludie. She does things just to aggravate me. Well, I hope she's happy now. She aggravated me. Now you take her hymn singin'. She never starts until I come into a room. And her poutin'! Why sometimes she goes a whole day just sittin' and starin' out the window. How would you like to spend twenty-four hours a day shut up with a woman that either sang hymns or looked out the window and pouted? You couldn't ignore it and don't tell me you could. No. There's only one thing to do, and that's to say "Quit it" every time she does something like that until she stops for good and all.

LUDIE: I'm not sayin' it's easy, Jessie Mae. I'm only sayin' . . .

JESSIE MAE: Well, let's change the subject. I don't want to get mad all over again. She keeps me so nervous never knowing when I leave whether she is going to try to run off to that old town or not.

LUDIE: Well, she's not going to run off again, Jessie Mae. She promised me she wouldn't.

JESSIE MAE: What she promised and . . .

LUDIE: Now, she can't run off. Her pension check hasn't come. You said yourself.

[MRS. WATTS *hears them. She lifts up the mattress on the daybed and takes out the pension check. She sits for a moment, looking at it, trying to decide whether to take this in to* JESSIE MAE. *She wraps it in a handkerchief and hides it under her dress.*]

JESSIE MAE: Well, I am not too sure that that check hasn't come. Sometimes I think she hides that check, and I tell you right now if it's not here tomorrow, I am going to search this house from top to bottom.

LUDIE: Well, I know the check will come tomorrow.

JESSIE MAE: I hope so. Rosella says she thinks it's terrible how close I have to stay here. Well, I told Rosella ever since your mother started that running-off business I don't feel easy going. I used to love it when I could get up from the breakfast table with an easy mind and go downtown and shop all morning, then get a sandwich and a Coke, or a salad at the cafeteria, see a picture show in the afternoon and then come home, that was fun. Shhh. I think I hear your mother still up.

[MRS. WATTS *is now sitting in her rocking chair, rocking and looking out the window.* LUDIE *comes into the living room.*]

LUDIE: Mama. Are you still up?

MRS. WATTS: Yes. I don't feel like sleeping, Ludie. You go on back to bed and don't worry about me.

LUDIE: All right, Mama.

[LUDIE *goes back to the bedroom.* JESSIE MAE *is at the dresser.*]

JESSIE MAE: Was she still up?

LUDIE [*passing her, goes to his side of the bed and sits*]: Yes.

JESSIE MAE: I knew it. I never get to go out of the house except for the beauty parlor. I'm not giving that up for anyone. I told Rosella that. I said no one was more faithful to a husband than I was to Ludie, when he was sick, but even then I went out to the beauty parlor once a week. I mean, I had to.

LUDIE: I wanted you to.

JESSIE MAE: I know you did.

[*Pause.* JESSIE MAE *goes and sits on her side of the bed.*]

That was a good supper we had tonight, wasn't it?

LUDIE: Uh-huh. Mama is a good cook.

JESSIE MAE: Yes. She is. I'll have to hand that to her. And an economical one. Well, she enjoys cooking. I guess you're born to enjoy it. I could never see how anyone could get any pleasure standing over a hot stove, but she seems to.

[*Pause.*]

Rosella asked me if I realized that it would be fifteen years this August since we were married. I hadn't realized it. Had you?

[LUDIE thinks for *a moment. He counts back over the years.*]

LUDIE: That's right, Jessie Mae. It'll be fifteen years this August.
JESSIE MAE: I hate to think of time going that fast.

[*Pause.*]

I never will forget the night I came home and told Rosella you had proposed. I thought you were the handsomest man alive.
LUDIE: And I thought you were the prettiest girl.
JESSIE MAE: Did you, Ludie? I guess I did have my good features. People used to tell me I looked like a cross between Joan Crawford and Clara Bow. And I thought you were the smartest man in the world. I still do. The thing that burns me up is that you don't let other people know it.
LUDIE: Jessie Mae, I've just got to start makin' some more money. I'm thinkin' about askin' for a raise. I'm entitled to it. I've been there six months now. I haven't been late or sick once. I've got to do it. I've got to ask for a raise tomorrow. I'm gonna walk into Mr. Douglas's office the first thing in the mornin' and I'm just gonna take the bull by the horns and I'm gonna say, "Mr. Douglas, I've got to have a raise starting as of now. We can't live on what you pay us. We have mother's pension check to help us out, and if we didn't have that, I don't know what we'd do."
JESSIE MAE: Well, I would.
LUDIE: I don't understand it, Jessie Mae. I try not to be bitter. I try not to . . . Oh, I don't know. All I know is that a man works eight years with a company. He saves a little money. He gets sick and has to spend two years in bed watching his savings all go. Then start all over again with a new company. Of course, the doctor says I shouldn't worry about it.

He says I've got to take things like they come. Every day, and that's what I try to do. But how can you help worryin' when you end up every month holding your breath to see if you're gonna make ends meet.

JESSIE MAE: You can't help being nervous. A lot of people get nervous.

[*She picks up the book.*]

What's this book?

LUDIE: I bought it at the drugstore coming home from the office.

JESSIE MAE: *How to Become an Executive.* What's that about?

LUDIE: It tells you how to prepare yourself for an executive position. It looks like there might be some helpful things in it.

[LUDIE *takes the book and leans back against the headboard of the bed again.* JESSIE MAE *restlessly looks around the room.*]

JESSIE MAE: You sleepy, Ludie?

LUDIE: No, not yet.

JESSIE MAE: I'm not either. I wish I had something good to eat. I wish the drugstore was open. We could get us some ice cream. I wish I had my movie magazine.

LUDIE: Where is it?

JESSIE MAE: In the living room.

LUDIE: I'll get it.

JESSIE MAE: No, honey, I don't want to get your mother awake. You rest. Rosella cried like her heart would break when she told me she couldn't have children.

[*Pause.*]

She wanted to know how I stood it not havin' children. I said I don't know about Ludie 'cause you can't always tell what he feels, but I stand it by never thinking about it. I have my own philosophy about those things, anyway. I feel things like that are in the hands of the Lord. Don't you, Ludie?

LUDIE: I guess so.

JESSIE MAE: I've been as good a wife to you as I know how. But if the Lord doesn't want to give us children, all the worryin' in the world won't help. Do you think?

LUDIE: No, it won't.

JESSIE MAE: Anyway, like I told Rosella, I don't have the money to be runnin' around the doctors about it, even if I wanted to.

LUDIE: Jessie Mae, if I get a raise, the first thing I want you to do is buy yourself a new dress.

JESSIE MAE: Well, thank you, Ludie. Besides, when you were sick, what would I have done if I'd had a bunch of kids to worry me? What are you thinking about?

LUDIE: This book.

JESSIE MAE: Ludie, do you ever think back over the past?

LUDIE: No.

JESSIE MAE: I don't either. I started today a little when Rosella brought up that fifteen-year business. But I think it's morbid. Your mother does that all the time.

LUDIE: My boss likes me. Billy Davidson told me today he was positive he did. Billy has been there ten years now, you know. He said he thought he liked my work a lot.

[*Pause.*]

Feelin' sleepy now?

JESSIE MAE: Uh-huh. Are you?

LUDIE [*getting off the bed and going to the bedroom door*]: Yes, I am.

[LUDIE *turns out the light, but instead of returning to bed he exits to the living room.* MRS. WATTS *is rocking back and forth in her rocker now, working her hands nervously.*]

LUDIE: Mama.

MRS. WATTS: I'm all right, Ludie. I'm just still not sleepy.

LUDIE: You're sure you're feelin' all right?

MRS. WATTS: Yes, I am.

LUDIE: Good night.

[LUDIE *starts out of the room.* MRS. WATTS *turns to him.*]

MRS. WATTS: Ludie, please, I want to go home.

LUDIE: Mama, you know I can't make a living there. We have to live in Houston.

MRS. WATTS: Ludie, son, I can't stay here any longer. I want to go home.
LUDIE: I beg you not to ask me that again. There's nothing I can do about it.

[LUDIE *goes back to the bedroom. He gets into bed.*]

JESSIE MAE: Was she still up?
LUDIE: Uh-huh. Good night.
JESSIE MAE: Good night.

[MRS. WATTS *quietly takes a suitcase down from the top of the wardrobe. She waits a moment, then takes some clothes from the drawer of the cupboard and puts them in the suitcase, and then she quietly closes it and puts the suitcase next to the wardrobe. She then goes back to her chair, sits, and is rocking back and forth as the lights fade.*]

SCENE 2

[*As the lights are brought up,* MRS. WATTS *is asleep in the rocker holding the check against her chest.* JESSIE MAE *is sitting on the edge of the bed, putting on stockings.* LUDIE *is in the kitchen.* MRS. WATTS *awakens, discovers the check, and nervously hides it under the rug. She looks out the window to see the time, runs over to Ludie's bedroom to see if he's awake, and runs out to the kitchen, calling as she goes.*]

MRS. WATTS: Ludie, it's eight-fifteen by the drugstore clock . . .
LUDIE [*calling back*]: Yes'm. Good morning, Mama.
MRS. WATTS: Good morning, son.

[LUDIE *enters with a cup of coffee.* MRS. WATTS *reenters the living room with a breakfast tray and dishes, singing a hymn to herself.*]

LUDIE: Did you get any sleep at all last night?
MRS. WATTS: Yes. Don't worry about me.

[*She continues her hymn singing.* JESSIE MAE *comes into the living room.*]

JESSIE MAE: It's too early for hymn singing.
MRS. WATTS: Good morning, Jessie Mae.
JESSIE MAE: Good morning, Mother Watts.

[JESSIE MAE *turns on the radio, which plays a popular song. She goes back into the bedroom. Calling from the bedroom:*] Ludie, turn that radio down, please, before they start knocking again.

LUDIE [*at the radio*]: Would you like me to turn it off?
JESSIE MAE [*calling*]: Oh, you might as well.
MRS. WATTS: I'll have your toast ready for you in a minute.

[MRS. WATTS *goes running out to the kitchen.*]

JESSIE MAE: Walk, don't run. I've just got to get me out of this house today, if no more than to ride downtown and back on the bus.
LUDIE [*finishing dressing*]: Why don't you?
JESSIE MAE: If Mother Watts's pension check comes I'll go to the beauty parlor. I'm just as tense. I think I've got a trip to the beauty parlor comin' to me.
LUDIE: You ought to go if the check comes or not. It doesn't cost that much.

[MRS. WATTS *comes in with the toast.*]

JESSIE MAE: Mother Watts, will you skip down and see if the mail has come yet? Your pension check ought to be here, and I want to get me to that beauty parlor.
MRS. WATTS: Yes, ma'am.

[MRS. WATTS *goes out for the mail at the outside door.* JESSIE MAE *looks after her suspiciously.*]

JESSIE MAE: Ludie, she's actin' silent again. Don't you think she's actin' silent again?
LUDIE: I hadn't noticed.

[LUDIE *take a last swig of his coffee.*]

JESSIE MAE: Well, she definitely is. You can say what you please, but to me it's always a sure sign she's gonna try and run off when she starts actin' silent.
LUDIE: She's not going to run off again, Jessie Mae. She promised me last time she wouldn't.

[LUDIE *starts up from the table.*]

JESSIE MAE: She just better not. What do you want, Ludie?

LUDIE: I want more coffee.

JESSIE MAE: Well, keep your seat. I'll get it.

LUDIE: No, I'll get it.

JESSIE MAE: No. I want to get it. You'll have a tiring day ahead of you. Now rest while you can.

[JESSIE MAE *goes out to the hallway for coffee.* MRS. WATTS *enters.*]

MRS. WATTS: Where's Jessie Mae?

LUDIE: In the kitchen.

MRS. WATTS [*calling out*]: There was no mail, Jessie Mae.

JESSIE MAE [*answering back from the kitchen*]: Had it been delivered yet?

MRS. WATTS: I don't know.

JESSIE MAE: Did you look in the other boxes to see if there was mail?

MRS. WATTS: No, ma'am. I didn't think to.

[MRS. WATTS *goes to the wardrobe and gets clothes to change into for the day. She goes to the bathroom to change her clothes.*]

LUDIE [*hollering as he goes to the bedroom for his coat and hat*]: I'll look on my way out. Why don't we have an early supper tonight? Six-thirty, if that's all right with you and Mama. After supper I'll take you both to the picture show.

[JESSIE MAE *comes into the bedroom with coffee.*]

JESSIE MAE: That's fine. What would you like to see, Ludie?

LUDIE: Whatever you want to see, Jessie Mae. You know best about picture shows.
[*Half to himself as he goes back to the living room followed by* JESSIE MAE:] I want to get to the office a little early this morning. Mr. Douglas is usually in by nine. I'd like a chance to talk to him before the others get there. I think I'm doin' the right thing, askin' for a raise. Don't you?

JESSIE MAE: Sure. I think I'll phone the beauty parlor for an appointment. I hope I can still get one.

[JESSIE MAE *goes to the phone on the desk.*]

Hello, Rita. This is Jessie Mae Watts. Can I have an appointment for my hair? The usual. Uh-huh.

[*She laughs.*]

Four o'clock. Nothin' earlier. All right. See you then.

[*She hangs up the phone.*]

Well, I can't get an appointment until four o'clock.

[MRS. WATTS *reenters and puts her bathrobe, nightgown, and slippers in the wardrobe.*]

LUDIE: I'm ready to go. Wish me luck on my raise.
JESSIE MAE: Good luck, Ludie.

[LUDIE *kisses her on the cheek.*]

MRS. WATTS: Good-bye, son.

[JESSIE MAE *follows* LUDIE *to the door leading to the stairs.* MRS. WATTS *goes to the bedroom and starts making the bed.*]

JESSIE MAE [*from offstage*]: Holler if there's any mail down there so we won't be runnin' up and down lookin' for mail that won't be there.
LUDIE [*calling back*]: All right.

[*The outside door is heard closing.*]

JESSIE MAE [*calling from the hallway*]: That pension check should have been here yesterday, shouldn't it, Mother Watts?
MRS. WATTS [*calling back and trying to seem unconcerned*]: I reckon so.
LUDIE [*calling from offstage downstairs*]: No mail for us.
JESSIE MAE [*now in the living room, calling down from the window*]: All right!
[*To* MRS. WATTS] I can't understand about that pension check, can you?
MRS. WATTS: No, ma'am.

[JESSIE MAE *casually takes* MRS. WATTS's *purse and looks inside. Finding nothing, she closes it and puts it back.*]

JESSIE MAE: I sure hope it isn't lost. You know you're so absentminded, you don't think you put it around the room someplace by mistake and forgot all about it.

[MRS. WATTS *rushes into the living room.*]

MRS. WATTS: I don't believe so.

[JESSIE MAE *looks around the room.* MRS. WATTS *watches anxiously everything she does.*]

JESSIE MAE: You know you said you lost that check once before, and it took us five days to find it. I came across it under this radio.

MRS. WATTS: I don't think I did that again, Jessie Mae.

[JESSIE MAE *begins a halfhearted search of the room, and when she gets to the corner of the rug where the check is hidden, she stoops as if to look under it, but it is only a strand of thread that has caught her attention.* JESSIE MAE *gives up the search.*]

JESSIE MAE: What could I do 'til four o'clock? What are you gonna do today?

MRS. WATTS: Well, I'm going to give the kitchen a good cleaning and put fresh paper on the shelves and clean the icebox.

JESSIE MAE: Well, I have a lot of things I have to do. I got some drawers I can straighten up.

[JESSIE MAE *goes into the bedroom.*]

Or maybe I'll put some flowers on that red dress of mine. If I wear the red dress tonight. I really don't know yet which dress I'm going to wear. Well, if I wear my red dress tonight, I'll wear this print one to the beauty parlor.

[JESSIE MAE *has taken a dress out of her closet and puts it on.* MRS. WATTS *takes out the check from under the rug and places it inside her dress and then starts into the kitchen.* JESSIE MAE *hears her running and calls to her.*]

Mother Watts!

MRS. WATTS: Yes, ma'am.

JESSIE MAE: There you go again. You never walk when you can run. You know it's none of my business, and I know you don't like me to suggest anything, but I don't think a woman your age should go running around a three-room apartment like a cyclone. It's really not necessary, Mother Watts. You never walk when you can run. I wish for once you would listen to me.

MRS. WATTS [*returning to the living room*]: I'm listening, Jessie Mae.

[JESSIE MAE *comes into the living room.*]

JESSIE MAE: You're not listening to a word. Mother Watts, are you feeling all right? You look a little pale.

MRS. WATTS: I'm feeling fine, Jessie Mae.

JESSIE MAE: Do you need anything from the drugstore?

MRS. WATTS: Just let me think a moment, Jessie Mae.

JESSIE MAE: Because if you do, I'd walk over to the drugstore and get
me a Coke. We don't need toothpaste. We don't need toothbrushes. I
got a bottle of Listerine yesterday. Can you think of anything we need
from the drugstore?

MRS. WATTS: Did you get that nail polish you mentioned?

JESSIE MAE: Oh, yes I have that. I hate to wait around here until four
o'clock. I think I'm gonna call Rosella and tell her to meet me at the
drugstore for a Coke.

[JESSIE MAE *goes to the phone and dials.* MRS. WATTS *is humming to herself.*]

Will you stop that hymn singing? Do you want me to jump right out
of my skin? You know what hymns do to my nerves.

[MRS. WATTS *stops humming.*]

And don't pout. You know I can't stand pouting.

MRS. WATTS: I didn't mean to pout, Jessie Mae. I only meant to be
silent.

JESSIE MAE [*hanging up the phone*]: Wouldn't you know it. She's not
home. I bet she's at the drugstore right now. I think I'll go on over to
the drugstore and just take a chance on Rosella's being there.

[JESSIE MAE *puts her hat on in the bedroom and grabs her purse.* MRS. WATTS
has gotten a hand sweeper from the kitchen and is sweeping around the room.]

I can't make up my mind what movie I want to see tonight. Well, I'll
ask Rosella. You know, when I first came to Houston, I went to see
three picture shows in one day. I went to the Kirby in the morning,
and the Metropolitan in the afternoon, and the Majestic that night.
People don't go see picture shows the way they used to.

[JESSIE MAE *comes back into the living room.*]

Well, I'm ready. Will you stop that noise for a minute. I'm nervous. I just want you to promise me one thing. That you won't put a foot out of this house and start that Bountiful business again. You'll kill Ludie if he has to chase all over Houston looking for you. And I'm warning you. The next time you run off, I'm calling the police. I don't care what Ludie says.

[JESSIE MAE *starts out of the room.*]

If Rosella calls, just tell her I'm at the drugstore.

[MRS. WATTS *has done her best to continue dusting the furniture during the latter speech, but she has been getting physically weaker and weaker. Finally, in a last desperate attempt to keep* JESSIE MAE *from noticing her weakness, she grabs hold again of the chair, trying to support herself. She sways and falls onto the daybed, just as* JESSIE MAE *is ready to leave the room.*]

Mother Watts . . .

[JESSIE MAE *runs to her. She is very frightened.*]

MRS. WATTS [*trying desperately to control herself*]: I'm all right, Jessie Mae.
JESSIE MAE: Is it your heart?
MRS. WATTS: No. Just a sinkin' spell. Just let me sit down for a minute and I'll be all right.
JESSIE MAE: Can I get you some water?
MRS. WATTS: Thank you.

[JESSIE MAE *starts to run into the kitchen for water, then turns back at the living room door.*]

JESSIE MAE: Do you want me to call a doctor?
MRS. WATTS: No, ma'am.
JESSIE MAE: Do you want me to call Ludie?
MRS. WATTS: No, ma'am.

[JESSIE MAE *continues to the kitchen and reenters the living room with a glass of water.* MRS. WATTS *drinks it.*]

JESSIE MAE: Are you feelin' better?

MRS. WATTS: Yes, I am, Jessie Mae.

[JESSIE MAE *takes the glass from* MRS. WATTS *and puts it on the desk.* MRS. WATTS *tries to get up.*]

JESSIE MAE: Do you think you ought to get up so soon?
MRS. WATTS: Yes, ma'am. I'm feeling much better already. I'll just sit back down.
JESSIE MAE: All right. I'll sit here for a while and keep you company.

[MRS. WATTS *sits on the daybed.* JESSIE MAE *sits in a chair.*]

How do you feel now?
MRS. WATTS: Better.
JESSIE MAE: That's good. It always scares the daylights out of me when you get one of those sinkin' spells. Of course, like I told you this morning, you wouldn't be having these sinkin' spells if you'd stop this running around. Well, it's your heart. If you don't want to take care of it no one can make you. But I tell you right now all I need is to have an invalid on my hands. I wish you'd think of Ludie. He's got enough to worry him without your gettin' down flat on your back.

[*The phone rings.* JESSIE MAE *goes to it.*]

Hello? . . . Oh, hello, Rosella. I tried to call you earlier. . . . Oh. You're at the drugstore. That's what I just figured. . . . Well, I'd like to, Rosella, but Mother Watts has had a sinking spell again and—
MRS. WATTS: Jessie Mae!
JESSIE MAE [*to Rosella*]: Hold on . . .
MRS. WATTS: You go on, Jessie Mae. I'm gonna be all right. I'll just rest here. There's nothing you can do for me.
JESSIE MAE: Are you sure?
MRS. WATTS: Yes, Jessie Mae, I'm sure.
JESSIE MAE: Well, all right then. Rosella, Mother Watts says she won't need me here. So I think I will come over for a little while. . . . All right. I'll see you in a few minutes. Good-bye.

[JESSIE MAE *hangs up the phone.*]

Now you're sure you'll be all right?
MRS. WATTS: Yes, ma'am.

JESSIE MAE: Well, then I'll go on over. Now you call me at the drugstore if you need me. You hear?

MRS. WATTS: Yes, ma'am.

[JESSIE MAE *goes out the entrance to the stairs.* MRS. WATTS *sits for a moment. Then she slowly and weakly gets up and goes to the door, listening. She is sure* JESSIE MAE *has gone.* MRS. WATTS *gets her suitcase from beside the wardrobe. Then she remembers the check, which she takes out, and sits at the table to endorse it. While* MRS. WATTS *is endorsing the check,* JESSIE MAE *comes running down the hall to her bedroom.*]

JESSIE MAE: I forgot to take any money along with me.

[JESSIE MAE *goes into the bedroom to get her money, which she takes from the dresser.* MRS. WATTS *has just enough time to stuff the check inside her dress, get the suitcase and put it back beside the wardrobe, and get writing paper from the desk before* JESSIE MAE *calls from the bedroom.*]

Who are you writing to?

MRS. WATTS: I thought I'd drop a line to Callie Davis, Jessie Mae. Let her know I'm still alive.

JESSIE MAE: Why did you decide to do that all of a sudden?

MRS. WATTS: No reason. The notion just struck me.

[JESSIE MAE *stops in the doorway of the living room.*]

JESSIE MAE: All right. But just in case you're trying to put something over on me with that pension check, I've told Mr. Reynolds at the grocery store never to cash anything for you.

[JESSIE MAE *exits.* MRS. WATTS *looks to see that* JESSIE MAE *is gone.* MRS. WATTS *picks up her purse, coat, and suitcase, and puts on her hat. She looks out the window to see that* JESSIE MAE *is on her way to the drugstore.* MRS. WATTS *leans against the table, having put down her suitcase to rest. As she rests, music cue begins (choral rendition of the hymn, "There's Not a Friend Like the Lowly Jesus"). The Houston apartment begins to move upstage; light is kept on* MRS. WATTS *leaning on the table. When the apartment, which is on a pallet, reaches its position, a light comes up on the now bare downstage area.* MRS. WATTS *picks up her suitcase and heads for the light. As she steps off the pallet, the music, now instrumental, slows to half tempo. As* MRS. WATTS *reaches a downstage position, a bench is pushed on by an old man from stage*] *right. He sets the bench in its proper position, tips his hat to* MRS. WATTS, *and continues offstage left. As he passes, a ticket booth with the* FIRST TICKET AGENT *inside appears from stage left wing. Next, two benches and a trash can, all on a pallet, slide from upstage right. All of this takes place to the music at half tempo.* MRS. WATTS *stands watching. The Houston bus station is created around her. Walls have tracked in, hiding the Houston apartment, becoming the walls of the bus station. It all seems somewhat miraculous—the beginning of an odyssey.*]

SCENE 3

[*The old man returns from stage left with a newspaper. He sits on the upstage bench. As he opens the newspaper, the music is replaced by the sounds of a mid-size city bus station. (The number of passengers entering and exiting throughout the scene depends on the resources of each particular production.) Full light bumps up, and* THELMA *enters from stage right and crosses to the* FIRST TICKET AGENT.]

FIRST TICKET AGENT: Yes?
THELMA: I want a ticket to Old Gulf, please.
FIRST TICKET AGENT: Yes, ma'am.

[*He reaches for a ticket.*]

Here you are. You change buses at Harrison.
THELMA: I know. How much, please?
FIRST TICKET AGENT: Four eighty.
THELMA: Yessir.

[*The* FIRST TICKET AGENT *hands* THELMA *her ticket.* MRS. WATTS *is so busy watching the doors that she doesn't notice it's her turn.*]

FIRST TICKET AGENT: Lady, it's your turn.

[*A couple enters stage right and gets in line behind* MRS. WATTS *at the ticket booth.*]

MRS. WATTS: Excuse me. I'd like a ticket to Bountiful, please.
FIRST TICKET AGENT: Where?
MRS. WATTS: Bountiful.
FIRST TICKET AGENT: What's it near?

MRS. WATTS: It's between Harrison and Cotton.

FIRST TICKET AGENT: Just a minute.

[*The* FIRST TICKET AGENT *takes a book from behind the window on a shelf. He looks inside it. A woman enters stage left and crosses to the stage right bench. She sits down and starts reading a magazine.* MRS. WATTS *is again watching the doors. The* FIRST TICKET AGENT *looks up.*]

Lady.

MRS. WATTS: Oh. Yessir.

FIRST TICKET AGENT: I can sell you a ticket to Harrison or to Cotton. But there's no Bountiful.

MRS. WATTS: Oh, yes there is, it's between—

FIRST TICKET AGENT: I'm sorry, lady. You say there is, but the book says there isn't. And the book don't lie.

MRS. WATTS: But . . . I . . .

FIRST TICKET AGENT [*impatiently*]: Make up your mind, lady. Cotton or Harrison. There are other people waiting.

MRS. WATTS: Well . . . Let me see . . . How much is a ticket to Harrison?

FIRST TICKET AGENT: Three fifty . . .

MRS. WATTS: Cotton?

FIRST TICKET AGENT: Four twenty.

MRS. WATTS: Oh, yes. Well, I'll have the one to Harrison, please.

FIRST TICKET AGENT: All right. That'll be three fifty, please.

MRS. WATTS: Yessir.

[MRS. WATTS *reaches for her pocketbook and is about to open it. She turns to the* FIRST TICKET AGENT.]

Can you cash a pension check? You see I decided to come at the last minute and I didn't have time to stop by the grocery store.

FIRST TICKET AGENT: I'm sorry, lady. I can't cash any checks.

MRS. WATTS: It's perfectly good. It's a government check.

FIRST TICKET AGENT: I'm sorry. It's against the rules to cash checks.

MRS. WATTS: Oh, is that so? I understand. A rule is a rule. How much was that again?

FIRST TICKET AGENT: Three fifty.

MRS. WATTS: Oh, yes. Three fifty. Just a minute, sir. I've got it all here in nickels and dimes and quarters.

[MRS. WATTS *opens her purse and takes a handkerchief out. The money is tied in the handkerchief. She unties it, places it on the counter, and begins to count out the amount for the ticket. She counts half aloud as she does it. She shoves a pile of silver toward the* FIRST TICKET AGENT.]

Here. I think this is three fifty.

FIRST TICKET AGENT: Thank you.

[*The* FIRST TICKET AGENT *rakes the money into his hand.* MRS. WATTS *ties her handkerchief back up.*]

MRS. WATTS: That's quite all right. I'm sorry to have taken up so much of your time.

[MRS. WATTS *picks up her suitcase and starts off.*]

FIRST TICKET AGENT: Here, lady. Don't forget your ticket.

[MRS. WATTS *comes running back.*]

MRS. WATTS: Oh, my heavens. Yes. I'd forget my head if it wasn't on my neck.

[MRS. WATTS *takes the ticket and goes away. The couple next in line steps up to the window.* MRS. WATTS *goes back to the entrance. She peeps out and then comes back into the bus station. She comes down to the bench.* THELMA *is seated there, reading. She looks up from her magazine. There is an empty space next to her.* MRS. WATTS *comes up to it.*]

Good evening.

THELMA: Good evening.

MRS. WATTS: Is this seat taken?

THELMA: No, ma'am.

MRS. WATTS: Are you expectin' anyone?

THELMA: No, ma'am

MRS. WATTS: May I sit here?

THELMA: Yes, ma'am.

[MRS. WATTS *puts the suitcase down along the side of the bench. The couple has finished buying tickets, and the woman exits stage left for the restroom. The man stands stage left of the benches.* MRS. WATTS *looks nervously around the station. All of a sudden she jumps up.*]

MRS. WATTS: Would you watch my suitcase, honey?

THELMA: Yes, ma'am.

MRS. WATTS: I'll be right back.

THELMA: Yes'm.

[MRS. WATTS *goes running back toward the door to the street.* THELMA *watches her go for a minute and then resumes reading her magazine. The* FIRST TICKET AGENT *is joined by the man who is to relieve him for the night. They greet each other and the* FIRST TICKET AGENT *leaves the bus station.* MRS. WATTS *comes back to the bench. She sits down and takes a handkerchief out of her purse. She wipes her forehead.*]

MRS. WATTS: Little warm, isn't it, when you are rushing around?

THELMA: Yes'm.

MRS. WATTS: I had to get myself ready in the biggest kind of hurry.

THELMA: Are you going on a trip?

MRS. WATTS: Yes, I am. I'm trying to get to a town nobody ever heard of around here.

THELMA: What town is it?

MRS. WATTS: Bountiful.

THELMA: Oh.

MRS. WATTS: Did you ever hear of it?

THELMA: No.

MRS. WATTS: You see. Nobody has. Well, it's not much of a town now, I guess. I haven't seen it myself in twenty years. But it used to be quite prosperous. All they have left is a post office and a filling station and a general store. At least they did when I left.

THELMA: Do your people live there?

MRS. WATTS: No. My people are all dead except my son and his wife, Jessie Mae. They live here in the city. I'm hurrying to see Bountiful before I die. I had a sinking spell this morning. I had to climb up on the bed and rest. It was my heart.

THELMA: Do you have a bad heart?

MRS. WATTS: Well, it's not what you call a good one. Doctor says it would last as long as I needed it if I could just cut out worrying. But it seems I can't do that lately.

[*She looks around the bus station again. She gets up out of her seat.*]

Excuse me. Would you keep your eye on that suitcase again?

THELMA: Yes, ma'am.

[MRS. WATTS *hurries back to the entrance of the bus station.* THELMA *picks up her magazine and goes back to reading.* MRS. WATTS *comes hurrying back to the seat. She doesn't sit down, but stands over by the side.*]

Lady. Is there anything wrong?

MRS. WATTS: No, honey. I'm just a little nervous. That's all.

[MRS. WATTS *hurries back toward the door. This time she opens it and goes outside.* THELMA *goes back to her reading. The woman enters from stage left and talks to the man.* MRS. WATTS *comes running back in. She hurries over to the seat and picks up the suitcase. The couple crosses stage right to the bench and sits next to the woman. In her confusion* MRS. WATTS *drops her handkerchief on the floor. Neither she nor* THELMA *sees it fall.*]

Say a prayer for me, honey. Good luck to you.

THELMA: Good luck to you.

[MRS. WATTS *goes running out toward the restroom.* LUDIE *and* JESSIE MAE *come in the outside door to the bus station. They stand a moment at the entrance, looking all around, and* JESSIE MAE *goes off toward the restroom.* LUDIE *wanders slowly down until he gets to stage left of the bench where* THELMA *is sitting. He pauses here, looking out in front of him and to each side.* JESSIE MAE *comes in. She walks over to* LUDIE.]

LUDIE: You want to sit down, Jessie Mae?

JESSIE MAE: Yes, I do. If you want to continue looking around, go ahead. I'll just wait over there.

[JESSIE MAE *goes and sits on the same bench as* THELMA.]

LUDIE: You checked the restroom carefully?

JESSIE MAE: Yes.

LUDIE: Want me to bring you a Coke?

JESSIE MAE: No.

LUDIE: Want me to buy you a movie magazine?

JESSIE MAE: Yes.

LUDIE: All right. I'll be right back.

[LUDIE *goes back out the outside door he came in, looking around as he goes.* JESSIE MAE *turns to* THELMA.]

JESSIE MAE: It's warm, isn't it?

[*The man crosses to the ticket booth to talk to the* SECOND TICKET AGENT.]

I hope you're lucky enough not to have to fool with any in-laws. I've got a mother-in-law about to drive me crazy. At least twice a year we have to try and keep her from getting on a train to go back to her hometown. Oh, she's so stubborn. I could just wring her neck. Her son spoils her, that's the whole trouble. She's just rotten spoiled. Do you live with your in-laws?

THELMA: No.

JESSIE MAE: Well, you're lucky. They're all stubborn. My husband is as stubborn as she is. I told Ludie at breakfast she had that silent look, and I bet she tries to run away. But no, he said she wouldn't because she has promised she wouldn't, and Ludie believes anything she says. I'm just worn out.

[*The man returns to the bench.*]

I've had my fourth Coca-Cola today, just to keep my spirits up. People ask me why I don't have any children. Why? I say I've got Ludie and Mother Watts. That's all the children I need.

[LUDIE *comes in with a movie magazine. He comes up to* JESSIE MAE.]

What did you bring me?

[*He shows her the magazine.*]

Oh, I've seen that one. Personally, I think we're wastin' our time here. She always tries to go by train.
LUDIE: But she can't go by train, Jessie Mae.
JESSIE MAE: She doesn't know that.
LUDIE: She's bound to by now.
JESSIE MAE: I tell you again, I think we ought to just turn this whole thing over to the police. That would scare her once and for all.
LUDIE: Well, I'm not going to call any police.

JESSIE MAE: It's for her own good. She's crazy.

LUDIE [*very angry with her*]: Now why do you talk like that? You know Mama isn't crazy.

[*Pause.*]

I just wish you wouldn't say things like that.

JESSIE MAE: Well you better do something. Let me tell you that, or she's gonna clonk out some place. She'll get to Bountiful and die from the excitement, and then we'll have all kinds of expenses bringing her body back here. Do you know what a thing like that could cost? Do you realize she had a sinkin' spell this mornin'?

LUDIE: I know. You've told me a hundred times. What can I do about it, Jessie Mae?

JESSIE MAE: I'm trying to tell you what you can do about it. Call the police.

LUDIE: I'm not going to call the police.

JESSIE MAE: Oh, you're not.

LUDIE: No.

JESSIE MAE: Then I think I will.

[JESSIE MAE *goes outside. The couple exits stage left, and the woman crosses to the ticket booth. After a brief conversation, she exits stage left.* LUDIE *looks around for a minute.* THELMA *has been watching the preceding scene. She has tried not to be seen by them, but she clearly has taken in every single word.* LUDIE *notices the magazine under his arm. He takes it in his hand and turns to* THELMA.]

LUDIE: Would you like this? I never read them, and my wife has seen it.

THELMA: Thank you.

[THELMA *takes the magazine and puts it in her lap. She goes back to her reading.* LUDIE *sits on the bench, looks on the floor, and sees the handkerchief that was dropped by* MRS. WATTS. *He reaches down and picks it up. He recognizes it. He gets up and goes running over to the ticket window.*]

LUDIE: Excuse me. Did an old lady come here and buy a ticket to a town named Bountiful?

SECOND TICKET AGENT: Where?

LUDIE: Bountiful!

SECOND TICKET AGENT: Not since I've been on duty.

LUDIE: How long have you been on duty?

SECOND TICKET AGENT: About five minutes.

LUDIE: Where is the man that was on before?

SECOND TICKET AGENT: He's gone home.

LUDIE: Oh.

[*He walks away, thinking what to do next. He sees* THELMA *and goes to her.*]

Excuse me, Miss.

THELMA: Yes?

LUDIE: I found this handkerchief here that belongs, I think, to my mother. She has a heart condition and it might be serious for her to be all alone. I don't think she has much money, and I'd like to find her. Do you remember having seen her?

THELMA: Well . . . I . . .

LUDIE: She'd be on her way to a town called Bountiful.

THELMA: Yes, I did see her. She was here talkin' to me. She left all of a sudden.

LUDIE: Thank you so much.

[JESSIE MAE *has come back in.*]

JESSIE MAE: Ludie.

[LUDIE *goes up to her.*]

LUDIE: I was right. She was here. The lady there said so.

JESSIE MAE: Well, it's too late now.

LUDIE: But this lady was talking to her.

JESSIE MAE: We're not going to wait. The police and I talked it over.

[THELMA *takes advantage of their argument to slip out of the station.*]

LUDIE [*turning on* JESSIE MAE]: You didn't really call them!

JESSIE MAE: I did, and they said in their opinion she was just trying to get our attention this way and we should just go home and pay her no mind at all.

LUDIE: How can I go home without Mama . . .

JESSIE MAE: The police tell me they have hundreds of cases like this every day. They say such things are very common among young people and old people.

LUDIE: Jessie Mae . . .

JESSIE MAE: Now, we're going to do what the police tell us to. They say she will come home when she's tired and hungry enough, and that makes a lot of sense to me. Now, Ludie, I wish you'd think of me for a change. . . . I'm not going to spend the rest of my life running after your mother.

LUDIE: All right, Jessie Mae.

[*He stands there, thinking.*]

JESSIE MAE: Now, come on, let's go. Come on.

[*She starts out.* LUDIE *pauses for a moment, thinking. He goes after her.*]

LUDIE: All right. But if Mama is not home in an hour, I'm going after her . . .

JESSIE MAE: Honestly, Ludie, you're so stubborn.

[*As* JESSIE MAE *and* LUDIE *exit stage right, the old man, who has been sitting reading his newspaper, gets up and pushes his bench offstage left. Lights fade and the bus station disappears.*]

SCENE 4

[*Out of the blackness, the bus seat, with* THELMA *and* MRS. WATTS, *floats downstage, stars appearing in the blackness framing the scene. Sounds of passing cars and trucks occur throughout the scene.*]

MRS. WATTS: Isn't it a small world? I didn't know we'd be on the same bus. Where do you go, honey?

THELMA: Harrison.

MRS. WATTS: Harrison!

THELMA: Yes. I change buses there.

MRS. WATTS: So do I go there. Isn't that nice? Is that a moving picture magazine?

THELMA: Yes, ma'am. Would you like to look at it?

MRS. WATTS: No, thank you.

[*She leans her head back on the seat and turns her head away.*]

The bus is nice to ride, isn't it?

THELMA: Yes. It is.

MRS. WATTS: I'm sorry I couldn't take a train, though.

THELMA: I tried to go by train, but you couldn't get connections tonight.

MRS. WATTS: I know. When I was a girl, I used to take excursions from Bountiful to Houston to Galveston. For the day, you know. Leave at five in the morning and return at ten that night. The whole town would come down to see you get off the train. I have such fond memories of those trips.

[*Pause. She looks over at* THELMA.]

Excuse me for getting personal, but what's a pretty girl like you doing traveling alone?

THELMA: My husband has just been sent overseas.

MRS. WATTS: Oh, I'm sorry to hear that.

THELMA: I'm going to stay with my family.

MRS. WATTS: Just say the Ninety-first Psalm over and over to yourself. It will be a bower of strength and protection for him.

[*She begins to recite with closed eyes.*]

"He that dwelleth in the secret place of the most high, shall abide under the shadow of the Almighty. I will say of the Lord, he is my refuge and my fortress: my God; in him will I trust. Surely he shall deliver thee from the fowler and the noisome pestilence. He shall cover thee with his feathers and under his wing shalt thou trust: his truth shall be thy shield and buckler."

[THELMA *covers her face with her hands—she is crying.* MRS. WATTS *looks up and sees her.*]

Oh, I'm sorry. I'm sorry, honey.

THELMA: That's all right. I'm just lonesome for him.

MRS. WATTS: Keep him under the Lord's wing, honey, and he'll be safe.

THELMA: Yes, ma'am.

[*She dries her eyes.*]

I'm sorry. I don't know what gets into me.

MRS. WATTS: Nobody needs be ashamed of crying. I guess we've all dampened our pillows sometime or other. I have, goodness knows.

THELMA: If I could only learn not to worry.

MRS. WATTS: I know. I guess we all ask that. Jessie Mae, my daughter-in-law, don't worry. "What for?" she says. Well, like I tell her, that's a fine attitude if you can cultivate it. Trouble is, I can't any longer.

THELMA: It is hard.

MRS. WATTS: I didn't use to worry. I was so carefree as a girl. Had lots to worry me, too. Everybody was so poor back in Bountiful. But we got along. I said to Papa once after our third crop failure in a row, "Whoever gave this place the name of Bountiful?" His papa did, he said, because in those days it was a land of plenty. You just had to drop seeds in the ground and the crops would spring up. Cotton and corn and sugarcane. I still think it's the prettiest place I know of. Jessie Mae says it's the ugliest. But she just says that, I know, to make me mad. She only saw it once, and then on a rainy day, at that. She says it's nothing but a swamp. "That may be," I said, "but it's a mighty pretty swamp to me." And then Sonny, that's my boy, Ludie, I call him Sonny, he said not to answer her back. He said it only caused arguments. And nobody ever won an argument with Jessie Mae, and I guess that's right.

[*Pause.* MRS. WATTS *looks out into space.*]

THELMA: Mrs. Watts . . .

MRS. WATTS: Yes?

THELMA: I think I ought to tell you this, . . . I . . . I don't want you to think I'm interfering in your business . . . but . . . well . . . you see, your son and your daughter-in-law came in just after you left . . .

MRS. WATTS: I know. I saw them coming. That's why I left so fast.

THELMA: Your son seems very concerned.

MRS. WATTS: Bless his heart.

THELMA: He found a handkerchief that you had dropped.

MRS. WATTS: Oh, mercy. That's right, I did.

THELMA: He asked me if I had seen you. I felt I had to say yes. I wouldn't have said anything if he hadn't asked me.

MRS. WATTS: Oh, that's all right. I would have done the same thing in your place. Did you talk to Jessie Mae?

THELMA: Yes.

MRS. WATTS: Isn't she a sight? I bet she told you I was crazy . . .

THELMA: Well . . .

MRS. WATTS: Oh, don't be afraid of hurting my feelings. Poor Jessie Mae, she thinks everybody's crazy that don't want to sit in the beauty parlor all day and drink Coca-Colas. She tells me a million times a day I'm crazy. That's the only time Ludie will talk back to her. He gets real mad when she calls me crazy. I think Ludie knows how I feel about getting back to Bountiful. Once when I was talkin' about somethin' we did back there in the old days, he just broke out cryin'. He was so overcome he had to leave the room.

[*Pause.* MRS. WATTS *starts to hum "There's Not a Friend Like the Lowly Jesus."*]

THELMA: That's a pretty hymn. What is the name of it?

MRS. WATTS: "There's Not a Friend Like the Lowly Jesus." Do you like hymns?

THELMA: Yes, I do.

MRS. WATTS: So do I. Jessie Mae says they've gone out of style . . . but I don't agree. I always sing one walking down the street or riding in the streetcar. Keeps my spirits up. What's your favorite hymn?

THELMA: Oh, I don't know.

MRS. WATTS: The one I was singin' is mine. I bet I sing it a hundred times a day. When Jessie Mae isn't home. Hymns make Jessie Mae nervous.

[*Pause.*]

Did Ludie mention my heart condition?

THELMA: Yes, he did.

MRS. WATTS: Poor Ludie. He worries about it so. I hated to leave him. Well, I hope he'll forgive me in time. So many people are nervous today. Ludie wasn't nervous back in Bountiful. Neither was I. The breeze from the Gulf would always quiet your nerves. You could sit on your front gallery and smell the ocean blowing in around you.

[*Pause.*]

I regret the day I left. But I thought it was the best thing at the time. Farming was so hard to make a living by and I had to see to the farm myself; our house was old, and there was no money to fix it with nor send Ludie to school. So I sold off the land and gave Ludie an education. Callie said I could always come back and visit her. She meant it, too. That's who I'm going to stay with now. Callie Davis. I get a card from her every Christmas. I wrote her last week and told her to expect me. Told her not to answer, though, on account of Jessie Mae opens all my mail. I didn't want her to know I was going. She'd try to stop me. Jessie Mae hates me. I don't know why, but she hates me.

[*Pause.*]

Hate me or not, I gotta get back and smell that salt air and work that dirt. I'm gonna spend the whole first month of my visit workin' in Callie's garden. I haven't had my hands in dirt in twenty years. My hands feel the need of dirt.

[*Pause.*]

Do you like to work the ground?

THELMA: I never have.

MRS. WATTS: Try it sometimes. It'll do wonders for you. I bet I'll live to be a hundred once I can get outside again. It was being cooped up in those two rooms that was killing me. I used to work the land like a man. Had to when Papa died. . . . I got two little babies buried there. Renee Sue and Douglas. Diphtheria got Renee Sue, I never knew what carried Douglas away. He was just weak from the start. I know Callie's kept their graves weeded. Oh, if my heart just holds out until I get there.

[*Pause.*]

Where do you go from Harrison?

THELMA: Old Gulf. My family have just moved there from Louisiana. I'll stay there with them until my husband comes home again.

MRS. WATTS: That's nice.

THELMA: It'll be funny living at home again.

MRS. WATTS: How long have you been married?

THELMA: A year. My husband was anxious for me to go. He said he'd worry about my being alone. I'm the only child, and my parents and I are very close.

MRS. WATTS: That's nice.

THELMA: My father being in the oil business, we've moved around a lot. I guess I went to school in fifteen different towns along the coast. I guess moving around like that made me and my mother and father even closer. I hoped so my mother and daddy would like my husband and he'd like them. I needn't have worried. They hit it off from the very first. Mother and Daddy say they feel like they have two children now. A son and a daughter.

MRS. WATTS: Isn't that nice? I've heard people say that when your son marries, you lose a son, but when your daughter marries, you get a son.

[*Pause.*]

What's your husband's name?

THELMA: Robert.

MRS. WATTS: That's a nice name.

THELMA: I think so. But I guess any name he had I would think was nice. I love my husband very much. Lots of girls I know think I'm silly about him, but I can't help it.

[*Pause.*]

MRS. WATTS: I wasn't in love with my husband.

[*Pause.*]

Do you believe we are punished for what we do wrong? I sometimes think that's why I've had all my trouble. I've talked to many a preacher about it; all but one said they didn't think so. But I can't see any other reason. Of course, I didn't lie to my husband. I told him I didn't love him, that I admired him, which I did, but I didn't love him. That I'd never love anybody but Ray John Murray as long as I lived, and I didn't, and I couldn't help it. Even after my husband died and I had to move back with Mama and Papa, I used to sit on the front gallery every morning and every evening just to nod hello to Ray John Murray as he went by the house to work at the store. He went a block out of his way to pass the house. He never loved nobody but me.

THELMA: Why didn't you marry him?

MRS. WATTS: His papa and my papa didn't speak. My papa forced me to write a letter saying I never wanted to see him again, and he got drunk and married out of spite. I felt sorry for his wife. She knew he never loved her.

[Pause.]

I don't think about those things anymore. But they're all part of Bountiful, and I guess that's why I'm starting to think of them again. You're lucky to be married to the man you love, honey.

THELMA: I know I am.

MRS. WATTS: Awfully lucky.

[Pause. MRS. WATTS looks out the window.]

Did you see that star fall over there?

THELMA: No.

MRS. WATTS: It was the prettiest thing I ever saw. You can make a wish on a falling star, honey.

THELMA: I know. It's too bad I didn't see it.

MRS. WATTS: You take my wish.

THELMA: Oh, no.

MRS. WATTS: Go on. I've gotten mine already. I'm on my way to Bountiful.

THELMA: Thank you.

[Pause. THELMA closes her eyes. MRS. WATTS watches her for a moment.]

MRS. WATTS: Did you make your wish?

THELMA: Yes, I did.

[MRS. WATTS leans her head back on the seat. She hums to herself. THELMA leans her head back, too. They close their eyes. The bus seat is pulled upstage as lights fade, leaving an area downstage right in dim light as the Harrison bus station—with ROY, the Harrison ticket agent, asleep in his cubicle—slides on.]

SCENE 5

[The bus's arrival is heard. ROY wakes up, turns on the overhead light, and checks his watch as he exits upstage left to meet the bus.]

ROY [*from offstage*]: Want any help with those bags?

THELMA [*entering*]: No, thank you.

ROY [*offstage, to* MRS. WATTS]: Good evening.

MRS. WATTS [*entering*]: Good evening.

VOICE OF BUS DRIVER [*offstage*]: Almost missed you.

ROY [*offstage*]: That'd be the first time for me.

VOICE OF BUS DRIVER [*offstage*]: Take it easy.

ROY [*offstage*]: All right, bye.

[THELMA *takes the bags and puts them down beside a bench. She goes over to* ROY.]

THELMA: Excuse me.

ROY: Yes?

THELMA: Is the bus to Old Gulf going to be on time?

ROY: Always is.

[THELMA *goes back to her seat near the suitcases.*]

MRS. WATTS [*to* THELMA]: What time is it, honey?

THELMA: Twelve o'clock.

MRS. WATTS: Twelve o'clock. I bet Callie will be surprised to see me walk in at twelve o'clock.

THELMA: Did you tell her you were coming today?

MRS. WATTS: No. I couldn't. Because I didn't know. I had to wait until Jessie Mae went to the drugstore.

THELMA: My bus is leaving in half an hour.

MRS. WATTS: Oh, I see. I guess I'd better be finding out how I'm going to get on out to Bountiful.

THELMA: You sit down. I'll ask the man.

MRS. WATTS: Thank you.

[MRS. WATTS *sits on the bench.* THELMA *turns to* ROY. *He is busy bringing in boxes left by the bus.*]

THELMA: Excuse me again.

ROY: Yes?

THELMA: My friend here wants to know how she can get to Bountiful.

ROY: Bountiful?

THELMA: Yes.

ROY: What's she going there for?

MRS. WATTS: I'm going to visit my girlhood friend.

ROY: I don't know who that's gonna be. The last person in Bountiful was Mrs. Callie Davis. She died day before yesterday. That is, they found her day before yesterday. She lived all alone, so they don't know exactly when she died.

MRS. WATTS: Callie Davis!

ROY: Yes, ma'am. They had the funeral this morning. Was she the one you were going to visit?

MRS. WATTS: Yessir, she was the one. She was my friend. My girlhood friend.

[MRS. WATTS *seems very old and tired and defeated.* THELMA *crosses to* ROY.]

THELMA: Is there a hotel here?

ROY: Yes'm. The Riverview.

THELMA: How far is it?

ROY: About five blocks.

THELMA: Is there a taxi around?

ROY: No, ma'am. Not this time of night.

THELMA: Thank you.

[ROY *goes back into the ticket window.* THELMA *goes over to* MRS. WATTS *at the bench. She speaks to her with great sympathy.*]

What'll you do now, Mrs. Watts?

MRS. WATTS: I'm thinking, honey. I'm thinking. It's come as quite a blow.

THELMA: I'm sorry. I'm so sorry.

MRS. WATTS: I know. I know.

[*Pause. Her strength and her will reviving*]

It's come to me what to do. I'll go on. That much has come to me. To go on. I feel my strength and my purpose strong within me. I'll go on to Bountiful. I'll walk those twelve miles if I have to.

THELMA: But if there's no one out there, what'll you do this time of night?

MRS. WATTS: Oh, yes. I guess that's right.

THELMA: I think you should wait until morning.

MRS. WATTS: Yes, I guess I should. Then I can hire someone to drive me out. You know what I'll do. I'll stay at my own house, or what's left of it. Put me in a garden. I'll get along fine with the help of my government checks.

THELMA: Mrs. Watts, the man says there's a hotel not too far away. I think you'd better let me take you there.

MRS. WATTS: Oh, no thank you. I wouldn't want to waste my money on a hotel. They're high as cats' backs, you know. I'll just sleep right here on this bench. Put my coat under my head, hold my purse under my arm.

[She puts the coat down on the bench like a pillow. She begins to look around for her purse. She has lost it.]

My purse!

[She begins to search frantically.]

Have you seen my purse, honey?

THELMA: Why, no.

[They begin to look around for it.]

MRS. WATTS: Oh, good heavens. I remember now. I left my purse on the bus.

THELMA: You're sure you left it there?

MRS. WATTS [joining her]: Yes. I am. I remember now. I didn't have it when I got off the bus. I kept thinkin' something was missin', but then I decided it was my suitcase that you had brought in for me. What am I gonna do, honey? All I have in the world is in that purse.

[THELMA goes back to the ticket window. ROY is drowsing.]

THELMA: Excuse me again.

ROY: Yeah?

THELMA: This lady left her purse on the bus.

ROY: All right. I'll call ahead. How can you identify it?

MRS. WATTS: It's a plain black purse.

ROY: How much money?

MRS. WATTS: Thirty-five cents and a pension check.

ROY: Who was the check made out to?

MRS. WATTS: To me, Mrs. Carrie Watts.

ROY: All right. I'll call up about it.

MRS. WATTS: Oh, thank you. You're most kind.

THELMA: How long will it take to get it back?

ROY: If I can get ahead of the bus at Don Tarle, I can get them to send it back on the Victoria bus and it should be here in a couple of hours.

MRS. WATTS: That's awful kind of you.

[ROY *picks up the phone and dials.*]

I don't know what I would have done without you.

THELMA: Try not to worry about the purse.

MRS. WATTS: I won't. I'm too tired to worry. Be time enough to start worrying when I wake up in the morning.

THELMA: Why don't you go on to sleep now if you can?

MRS. WATTS: Oh, I thought I'd stay up and see you off.

THELMA: No. You go on to sleep.

MRS. WATTS: I couldn't go right off to sleep now. I'm too wound up. You know I don't go on a trip every day of my life.

ROY: You're lucky. Bus hadn't gotten to Don Tarle yet. If they can find the purse, it'll be here around five.

MRS. WATTS: Thank you. Thank you so much.

THELMA: Make you feel better?

MRS. WATTS: Yes, it does. Of course, everything has seemed to work out today. Why is it some days everything works out, and some days nothing works out. What I mean is, I've been trying to get on that bus for Bountiful for over five years. Usually Jessie Mae and Ludie find me before I ever get inside the railroad station good. Today, I got inside both the railroad station and the bus station. Bought a ticket, seen Ludie and Jessie Mae before they saw me. Hid out. Met a pretty friend like you. Lost my purse, and now I'm having it found for me. I guess the good Lord is just with me today.

[*Pause.*]

I wonder why the Lord isn't with us every day? It would be so nice if he was. Well, maybe then we wouldn't appreciate so much the days when he's on our side. Or maybe he's always on our side and we don't know it. Maybe I had to wait twenty years cooped up in a city before I could appreciate getting back here.

[*Pause.* THELMA *rests her head back on the bench.* MRS. WATTS *rests her head. She hums her hymn.*]

It's so nice being able to sing a hymn when you want to. I'm a happy woman, young lady. A very happy woman.

THELMA: I still have a sandwich left. Will you have one?

[THELMA *gets the sandwich from her suitcase and unwraps it.*]

MRS. WATTS: Sure you don't want it?

THELMA: No, I'm full.

MRS. WATTS: Then I'll have a half, thank you.

THELMA: Take the whole sandwich. I'm not hungry.

MRS. WATTS: No, thank you. Just half. You know, I don't eat much. Particularly if I'm excited.

[*She rises, nibbling on the sandwich, and walks to just outside the door.* THELMA *follows.*]

You know, I came to my first dance in this town.

THELMA: Did you?

MRS. WATTS: Yes, ma'am. It was the summertime. My father couldn't decide if he thought dancin' was right or not. But my mother said she had danced when she was a girl and I was gonna dance. And so I went. The girls from all over the county came for this dance. It was at the Opera House. I forget what the occasion was. Somethin' special, though.

[*Pause. She looks at* THELMA.]

Do you know something, young lady? If my daughter had lived, I would have wanted her to be just like you.

THELMA: Oh, thank you.

MRS. WATTS [*with great tenderness*]: Just like you. Sweet and considerate and thoughtful.

THELMA: Oh, no . . . I'm . . .

MRS. WATTS: Oh, yes. Sweet and considerate and thoughtful. And pretty.

THELMA: Well, thank you.

[*Pause.*]

Mrs. Watts . . . I hope you don't mind my askin' this, but I worry about your son. Are you going to let him know where you are?

MRS. WATTS: Oh, yes, ma'am. As soon as I get that check cashed, I'm going to send him a telegram. [*To* ROY] I was tellin' my little friend here that I came to my first dance in this town.

ROY: Is that so?

MRS. WATTS: Yes. And I've been to Harrison quite a few times in my life, shopping.

ROY [*to* THELMA]: You'd better get outside, Miss. Bus will be up the road. It won't wait this time of night unless it sees we have a passenger.

THELMA: All right.

[*She gets her suitcase.*]

Good-bye, Mrs. Watts.

MRS. WATTS [*following her to the door*]: Good-bye, honey. Good luck to you. And thank you for everything.

THELMA: That's all right. Good luck to you.

MRS. WATTS: Thank you.

[THELMA *kisses her.* THELMA *goes out into the night, followed by* ROY. MRS. WATTS *watches* THELMA. *Offstage a bus is heard pulling up.*]

VOICE OF BUS DRIVER [*offstage*]: Everything all right?

ROY [*offstage*]: Everything's just fine.

VOICE OF BUS DRIVER [*offstage*]: See ya tomorrow.

ROY [*offstage*]: All right. Bye.

[MRS. WATTS *waves. The bus is heard leaving.* ROY *and* MRS. WATTS *come back inside the bus station.*]

Are you gonna stay here all night?

MRS. WATTS: I have to. Everything I have is in that purse and we can't go anyplace without money.

ROY: I guess that's right.

[*He starts away.*]

MRS. WATTS: Do they still have dances in Borden's Opera House?

ROY: No, ma'am. It's torn down. They condemned it, you know.

[*He starts on. He pauses.*]

Did you ever know anybody in Harrison?

MRS. WATTS: I knew a few people when I was girl. Priscilla Nytelle. Did you know her?

ROY: No, ma'am.

MRS. WATTS: Nancy Lee Goodhue?

ROY: No, ma'am.

MRS. WATTS: The Fay girls?

ROY: No, ma'am.

MRS. WATTS: I used to trade in Mr. Ewing's store. I knew him to speak to.

ROY: Which Ewing was that?

MRS. WATTS: George White Ewing.

ROY: He's dead.

MRS. WATTS: Is that so?

ROY: Been dead for twelve years.

MRS. WATTS: Is that so?

ROY: He left quite a bit of money, but his son took over his store and lost it all. Drank.

MRS. WATTS: Is that so? One thing I can say about my boy is that he never gave me any worry that way.

ROY: Well, that's good. I've got one boy that drinks and one boy that doesn't. I can't understand it. I raised them the same way.

MRS. WATTS: I know. I've known of other cases like that. One drinks. The other doesn't.

ROY: A friend of mine has a girl that drinks. I think that's the saddest thing in the world.

MRS. WATTS: Isn't it?

[*Pause.*]

ROY: Well. Good night.

MRS. WATTS: Good night.

[ROY *stands waiting to switch off the light while* MRS. WATTS *takes her suitcase and coat and makes a bed for herself on the bench. She lies down. He goes inside the ticket booth. He sticks his head out the cage.*]

ROY: Good night.
MRS. WATTS: Good night.

[ROY *turns off the light inside the ticket window.* MRS. WATTS *is humming quietly to herself. Her humming fades away as the lights fade out.*]

SCENE 6

[*The lights are brought up.* ROY *is in his cubicle sound asleep and snoring slightly. The* SHERIFF *comes in. He stands by the door for a moment, looking around the bus station. He sees* MRS. WATTS *lying on the bench asleep. He goes over to her and looks down. He stands for a moment watching her sleep. He looks over at the ticket window and sees that* ROY *is asleep. The* SHERIFF *goes over to* ROY *and shakes him.*]

SHERIFF: Come on, Roy, wake up.
ROY: Yeah?

[*He opens his eyes. He sees the* SHERIFF *and comes out.*]

Oh, hello, Sheriff.
SHERIFF: How long has that old woman been here?
ROY: About four hours.
SHERIFF: Did she get off the bus from Houston?
ROY: Yessir. I know her name. It's Watts. She left her purse on the bus, and I had to call up to Don Tarle about it.
SHERIFF: Have you got her purse?
ROY: Yes, it just came.
SHERIFF: She's the one, all right. I've had a call from the Houston police to hold her until her son can come for her.
ROY: She said she used to live in Bountiful.
SHERIFF: Yeah. I believe I remember some Watts a long time ago over that way. I think that old ramshackly house about to fall into the Brazos River belonged to them.
ROY: That right? They must have been before my time. What do the police want her for?

SHERIFF: Police don't. It's her son. He wants to take her back home. Claims she's not responsible. Did she act crazy to you?

ROY: Not that I noticed. Is she crazy?

SHERIFF: They say so.

[*He starts over to her to wake her up. He stands, looking at her for a moment. He comes back to* ROY.]

Poor old thing. She's sleeping so sound. I don't have the heart to wake her up. I'll tell you what, I'll go down and call Houston . . . tell them she's here. Her son is coming in his car. He should be here around seven-thirty. I'll be back in ten minutes. If she gives you any trouble, just call me. Keep your eye on her.

ROY: All right.

[*The* SHERIFF *goes out.* MRS. WATTS *wakes up. She opens her eyes. She looks around, trying to remember where she is. Then she sees* ROY.]

MRS. WATTS: Good morning.

ROY: Good morning.

MRS. WATTS: Could you tell me the time?

ROY: It's around four-thirty.

MRS. WATTS: Thank you. Did my purse arrive?

ROY: Yes, ma'am.

[ROY *reaches under the ticket window and hands the purse to her.*]

MRS. WATTS: Thank you so much. I wonder if you could cash a check for me?

ROY: I'm sorry. I can't.

MRS. WATTS: It's a government check, and I have identification.

ROY: I'm sorry. I can't.

MRS. WATTS: Do you know where I could get a check cashed?

ROY: Why?

MRS. WATTS: I need money to get me started in Bountiful. I want to hire someone to drive me out there and look at my house and get a few groceries. Try to find a cot to sleep on.

ROY: I'm sorry, lady. You're not going to Bountiful.

MRS. WATTS: Oh, yes, I am. You see . . .

ROY: I'm sorry, lady. You're not going anyplace right now. I have to hold you here for the sheriff.

MRS. WATTS: The sheriff?

ROY: Yes, ma'am.

MRS. WATTS: You're joking with me!? Don't joke with me. I've come too far.

ROY: I'm sorry. That's how it is.

MRS. WATTS: What has the sheriff got to do with me?

ROY: He came a few minutes ago while you were asleep and said I was to keep you here until your son arrived in his car this morning.

MRS. WATTS: My son hasn't got a car, so I don't believe you. I don't believe you.

ROY: It's the truth. He'll be here in a little while, and you can ask him yourself.

[*Pause.*]

MRS. WATTS: Then you're not joking?

ROY: No.

[MRS. WATTS *takes her coat and suitcase and runs for the entrance.* ROY *senses what she is going to do and gets there first—blocking her way.*]

MRS. WATTS: All right. But I'm going, do you understand? You'll see. This is a free country. And I'll tell him that. No sheriff or king or president will keep me from going back to Bountiful.

ROY: All right. You tell him that.

MRS. WATTS: What time is my son expected?

ROY: Sheriff says around seven-thirty.

MRS. WATTS: What time is it now?

ROY: I told you around four-thirty.

MRS. WATTS: Where can I get me a driver?

ROY: Ma'am?

MRS. WATTS: If you can get me a driver, I can make it to Bountiful and back before seven-thirty . . .

ROY: Look, lady . . .

MRS. WATTS: That's all I want. That's all I ask. Just to see it. To stand on the porch of my own house, once more. Walk under the trees. I swear I would come back then meek as a lamb.

ROY: Lady . . .

MRS. WATTS: Last night, I thought I had to stay. I thought I'd die if I couldn't stay. But I'll settle for less now. Much, much less. An hour. A half-hour. Fifteen minutes.

ROY: Lady, it ain't up to me. I told you, the sheriff—

MRS. WATTS [*screaming*]: Then get me the sheriff.

ROY: Look, lady . . .

MRS. WATTS: Get me the sheriff. The time is going. They'll have me locked in those two rooms again soon. The time is going . . . the time is . . .

[*The* SHERIFF *comes in. The* SHERIFF *goes over to* MRS. WATTS.]

SHERIFF: Mrs. Watts?

MRS. WATTS: Yessir.

[*She looks up at him. She puts the coat and suitcase down.*]

Are you the sheriff?

SHERIFF: Yes, ma'am.

MRS. WATTS: I understand my son will be here at seven-thirty to take me back to Houston.

SHERIFF: Yes, ma'am.

MRS. WATTS: Then listen to me, sir. I've waited a long time. Just to get to Bountiful. Twenty years I've been walkin' the streets of the city, lost and grieving. And as I've grown older and my time approaches, I've made one promise to myself, to see my home again . . . before I die . . .

SHERIFF: Lady . . . I . . .

MRS. WATTS: I'm not asking that I not go back. I'm willing to go back. Only let me travel these twelve miles first. I have money. I can pay . . .

SHERIFF: I think that's between you and your son.

MRS. WATTS: Ludie? Why, he's got to do whatever Jessie Mae tells him to. I know why she wants me back. It's for my government check.

SHERIFF: I don't know anything about that. That's between you and your son.

MRS. WATTS: Won't you let me go?

SHERIFF: No. Not unless your son takes you.

MRS. WATTS: All right. Then I've lost. I've come all this way only to lose. I've kept thinking back there day and night in those two rooms, I kept

thinkin' . . . and it may mean nothin' at all to you, but I kept thinkin'
. . . that if I could just set foot there for a minute . . . even . . . a second . . . I might get some understanding of why . . . why my life has grown so empty and meaningless. Why I've turned into a hateful, quarrelsome old woman. And before I leave this earth, I'd like to recover some of the dignity . . . the peace I used to know. For I'm going to die . . . and Jessie Mae knows that . . . and she's willful, and it's her will I die in those two rooms. Well, she won't have her way. It's my will to die in Bountiful.

SHERIFF: Mrs. Watts.

MRS. WATTS: Let me go those twelve miles . . . before it's too late. Understand me. Suffering I don't mind. Suffering I understand. I never protested once. Though my heart was broken when those babies died. I could stand seeing the man I love walk through life with another woman. But this fifteen years of bickering. Endless, petty bickering . . . It's made me like Jessie Mae sees me. It's ugly, I won't be that way. I want to go home. I want to go home. I want to go . . .

[*She is unable to speak any more. She is on the verge of collapse.*]

SHERIFF: Roy, hurry. Call a doctor.

[MRS. WATTS *summons up her last bit of strength to get free.*]

MRS. WATTS: No. No doctor. Bountiful . . . Bountiful . . . Bountiful . . .

[MRS. WATTS *has collapsed and the* SHERIFF *catches her on bended knee. They are surrounded by a pool of light. A short pause. Then, music cue comes in and the Harrison bus station, with* ROY *in his cubicle, slides stage right.*]

SCENE 7

[*As the station goes offstage,* MRS. WATTS *starts to revive. The* SHERIFF *stands and offers his hands, which* MRS. WATTS *takes, pulling herself to her feet. The Harrison set is now offstage and the back wall is ready to open and reveal Bountiful, bathed in early morning light and birdsong.*]

MRS. WATTS: I'm home, I'm home. I'm home. Thank you. I thank you. I thank you. I thank you.

[*They pause for a moment in the yard.* MRS. WATTS *is obviously still quite weak.*]

SHERIFF: You'd better sit down and rest for a while. You don't want to overdo it.

MRS. WATTS: Yessir.

[*She sits on a tree stump in the yard.*]

SHERIFF: Feeling all right?

MRS. WATTS: Yes, I am. I feel ever so much better.

SHERIFF: You look better. I hope I've done the right thing in bringing you here. Well, I don't see what harm it can do. As long as you mind the doctor and don't get overexcited.

MRS. WATTS: Yessir.

SHERIFF: Soon as you've rested for a little I'll go on back to my car and leave you alone. You can call me if you need anything. I'll stay out here until your son arrives.

MRS. WATTS: Thank you. You've been very kind.

[*A bird calls.* MRS. WATTS *and the* SHERIFF *sit listening to it. It whistles once again.*]

What kind of a bird was that?

SHERIFF: Redbird.

MRS. WATTS: I thought that was a redbird, but I hadn't heard one in so long, I couldn't be sure.

[*Pause.*]

Do they still have scissortails around here?

SHERIFF: Yes, ma'am. I still see one every once in a while when I'm driving around the country.

MRS. WATTS: I don't know of anything prettier than a scissortail flying around in the sky.

[*Pause.*]

My father was a good man in many ways, a peculiar man, but a good one. One of the things he couldn't stand was to see a bird shot on his land. If men came here hunting, he'd take a gun and chase them away.

I think the birds knew they couldn't be touched here. Our land was always a home to them. Ducks and geese and finches and blue jays. Bluebirds and redbirds. Wild canaries and blackbirds and mockers and doves and ricebirds . . .

SHERIFF: Ricebirds are gettin' thicker every year. They seem to thrive out here on the coast.

MRS. WATTS: I guess a mockin' bird is my favorite of them all.

SHERIFF: I guess it's mine, too.

MRS. WATTS: I don't know, though. I'm mighty partial to a scissortail. I hope I get to see one soon.

SHERIFF: I hope you can.

MRS. WATTS: My father was born on this land and in this house. Did you know my father?

SHERIFF: No, ma'am. Not that I can remember.

MRS. WATTS: I guess there are not many around here that remember my father. I do, of course, and my son. Maybe some old-timers around Harrison.

[Pause.]

It's funny, ever since I've been here I've been half expectin' my father and my mother to walk out of the house and greet me and welcome me home. When you've lived longer than your house and your family, you've lived too long.

[Pause.]

Or maybe it's just me. Maybe the need to belong to a house and a family and a town has gone from the rest of the world.

SHERIFF: How big was your farm, Mrs. Watts?

MRS. WATTS: Three hundred and seventy-five acres were left when my papa died, and I sold off all but the house and the yard.

[Pause.]

You say the store burned down fifteen years ago?

SHERIFF: Yes, ma'am. What was left of it. You see with the good roads we have now in the county, the little towns and their country stores are all disappearing. The farmers ride into Cotton or Harrison to trade . . .

MRS. WATTS: But what's happened to the farms? For the last five miles I've seen nothing but woods . . .

SHERIFF: I know. The land around Bountiful just played out. People like you got discouraged and moved away, sold off the land for what they could get. H. T. Mavis bought most of it up. He let it go back into timber. He keeps a few head of cattle out here. That's about all . . .

MRS. WATTS: Callie Davis kept her farm going.

SHERIFF: Yes. She did. She learned how to treat her land right, and it began paying off for her toward the end. I've heard she was out riding her tractor the day before she died. Lonely death she had. All by herself in that big house.

MRS. WATTS: There are worse things.

SHERIFF: Looks to me like you're going to have a pretty day.

MRS. WATTS: I hope so. My daughter-in-law has never seen our place in the sunshine. I expect my son will bring her along with him. I'd hate for her to have to see it again in the rain.

SHERIFF: Feeling more rested now?

MRS. WATTS: Oh, yes, I am.

SHERIFF: Good. Then I'll be getting on back to my car. You just call me if you need anything.

MRS. WATTS: Thank you. You'll never know what this has meant to me.

SHERIFF: Glad I could oblige.

[*He gets up and walks to the corner of the yard. Just before he goes out, he turns and waves.* MRS. WATTS *waves back to him. When he is out of sight, she rises slowly, walks over to the house, and steps up onto the porch. She slowly walks along the porch and into the house. The sun comes up full now, filling the stage with light.* LUDIE *enters. He goes toward the house, pauses, looks around.*]

LUDIE: Mama,

[*Pause.*]

Mama.

[*A pause, he panics.*]

Mama!

[MRS. WATTS *comes out of the house.*]

Hello, Mama.

MRS. WATTS: Hello, son.

LUDIE: How do you feel?

MRS. WATTS: I'm feelin' better, Ludie.

LUDIE: That's good. They told me at the bus station you had another attack.

MRS. WATTS: Yes, I did. All the excitement, I guess. But I feel fine now.

LUDIE: Yes'm.

MRS. WATTS: I got my wish.

LUDIE: Yes'm.

[LUDIE *walks away from the porch down to the corner of the yard.* MRS. WATTS *follows him.*]

MRS. WATTS: I hope I didn't worry you too much, Ludie. But I just felt I had to . . .

LUDIE: I know, Mama.

MRS. WATTS: You see, son, I know it's hard for you to understand and Jessie Mae . . . understand—but . . .

LUDIE: Yes, ma'am. I understand, Mama. It's done now. So let's forget about it.

MRS. WATTS: All right, Sonny.

[*Pause.*]

You did bring Jessie Mae, didn't you?

LUDIE: Yes, ma'am.

MRS. WATTS: Well, now she's here isn't she going to get out of the car and look around a little?

LUDIE: She didn't seem to want to, Mama.

MRS. WATTS: You asked her?

LUDIE: Yes, ma'am.

[*Pause.*]

MRS. WATTS: Did you ask about your raise, son?

LUDIE: Yes, ma'am, and Mr. Douglas told me he liked my work and he'd be glad to recommend a raise for me.

MRS. WATTS: Oh.

[*Pause.*]

The sky's so blue, Ludie. Did you ever see the sky so blue?

LUDIE: No, ma'am.

MRS. WATTS: Callie Davis died.

LUDIE: Is that so? When did that happen?

MRS. WATTS: They don't rightly know. They found her dead. She'd been ridin' a tractor the day before they found her. Buried her yesterday.

[*Pause.*]

LUDIE: Mama, I should have made myself bring you here before. I'm sorry, but I thought it would be easier for both of us not to see the house again.

MRS. WATTS: I know, Ludie.

[*Pause.*]

Now you're here, wouldn't you like to come inside, son, and look around?

LUDIE: I don't think I'd better, Mama. I don't see any use in it. It would just make me feel bad. I'd rather remember it like it was.

[*Pause.* MRS. WATTS *looks at the house. She smiles.*]

MRS. WATTS: The old house has gotten kind of rundown, hasn't it?

LUDIE: Yes, it has.

[MRS. WATTS *starts back toward the house slowly.*]

MRS. WATTS: I don't think it'll last out the next Gulf storm.

LUDIE: It doesn't look like it would.

[MRS. WATTS *turns and looks at* LUDIE *standing in the yard.*]

MRS. WATTS: You know who you look like standing there, Ludie?

LUDIE: Who?

MRS. WATTS: My papa.

LUDIE: Do I?

MRS. WATTS: Just like him. Of course, I've been noticing as you grow older you look more and more like him. My papa was a good-looking man.

LUDIE: Was he?

MRS. WATTS: You've seen his pictures. Didn't you think so?

LUDIE: I don't remember. It's been so long since I looked at his picture.

MRS. WATTS: Well, he was always considered a very nice-looking man.

[*Pause.*]

Do you remember my papa at all, son?

LUDIE: No, ma'am. Not too well. I was only ten when he died, Mama. I remember the day he died. I heard about it as I was coming home from school. Lee Weems told me. I thought he was joking and I called him a liar. I remember you takin' me into the front room there the day of the funeral to say good-bye to him. I remember the coffin and the people sitting in the room. Old man Joe Weems took me up on his knee and told me that Grandpapa was his best friend and that his life was a real example for me to follow. I remember Grandmama sitting by the coffin crying, and she made me promise that when I had a son of my own, I'd name it after Grandpapa. I would have, too. I've never forgotten that promise.

[*Pause.*]

Well, I didn't have a son. Or a daughter.

[*Pause.*]

Billy Davidson told me his wife is expecting her fourth child. They have two girls and a boy, now. Billy Davidson doesn't make much more than I do, and they certainly seem to get along. Own their own home and have a car. It does your heart good to hear them tell about how they all get along. Everybody has their own job, even the youngest child. She's only three. She puts the napkins around the table at mealtimes. That's her job. Billy said to me, "Ludie, I don't know how I'd keep going without my kids." He said, "I don't understand what keeps you going, Ludie. What you work for." I said, "Well, Billy . . ." Oh, Mama, I haven't made any kind of life for you, either one of you, and I try so hard. I try so hard. Oh, Mama. I lied to you. I do remember. I remember so much. This house. The life here. The night you woke me up and dressed me and took me for a walk when there was a full moon and I cried because I was afraid and you comforted me. Mama, I want to stop remembering . . . It doesn't do any good to remember.

[*A car horn is heard in the distance—loud and impatient.* LUDIE *looks in the direction of the horn.*]

That's Jessie Mae.

MRS. WATTS: Whose car did you come in?

LUDIE: I borrowed Billy Davidson's car. He didn't want me to have it at first. You know people are funny about lending their car, but then I explained what happened and he was nice about it.

[*The car horn is heard again.*]

We have to start back now, Mama. Jessie Mae is nervous that I might lose my job.

MRS. WATTS [*frantically trying to find an excuse not to leave*]: Didn't you ask for the day off?

LUDIE: No, ma'am. I only asked for the morning off.

MRS. WATTS: What time is it now?

LUDIE: Must be after eight. We were a little late getting here.

MRS. WATTS: We can drive it in three hours, can't we, Ludie?

LUDIE: Yes, ma'am, but we might have a flat or run into traffic or something. Besides, I promised Billy I'd get his car back to him by twelve.

MRS. WATTS: Son, why am I going back at all? Why can't I stay?

LUDIE: Mama, you can't stay.

MRS. WATTS: Ludie.

LUDIE: You know that.

MRS. WATTS: Ludie.

LUDIE: Now come on.

[MRS. WATTS *cries passionately, openly, bitterly.*]

MRS. WATTS: Ludie. Ludie. What's happened to us? Why have we come to this?

LUDIE: I don't know, Mama.

MRS. WATTS: To have stayed and fought the land would have been better than this.

LUDIE: Yes'm.

MRS. WATTS: Pretty soon it'll all be gone. Ten years . . . twenty . . . this house . . . me . . . you . . .

LUDIE: I know, Mama.

[*Pause.* MRS. WATTS *looks into* LUDIE*'s suffering face. She looks around. She speaks with great tenderness.*]

MRS. WATTS: But the river will be here. The fields. The woods. The smell of the Gulf. That's what I always took my strength from, Ludie. Not from houses, not from people. It's so quiet. It's so eternally quiet. I had forgotten the peace. The quiet. And it's given me strength once more, Ludie. To go on and do what I have to do. I've found my dignity and my strength.

LUDIE: I'm glad, Mama.

MRS. WATTS: And I'll never fight with Jessie Mae again or complain. Do you remember how my papa always had that field over there planted in cotton?

LUDIE: Yes, ma'am.

MRS. WATTS: See, it's all woods now. But I expect someday people will come again and cut down the trees and plant the cotton and maybe even wear out the land again and then their children will sell it and go to the cities and then the trees will come up again.

LUDIE: I expect so, Mama.

MRS. WATTS: We're part of all this. We left it, but we can never lose what it has given us.

LUDIE: I expect so, Mama.

[JESSIE MAE *enters.*]

JESSIE MAE: Ludie. Are you coming or not?

LUDIE: We were just startin', Jessie Mae.

MRS. WATTS: Hello, Jessie Mae.

JESSIE MAE: I'm not speakin' to you. I guess you're proud of the time you gave us. Dragging us all the way out here this time of the mornin'. If Ludie loses his job over this, I hope you're satisfied.

LUDIE: I'm not goin' to lose my job, Jessie Mae.

JESSIE MAE: Well, you could.

LUDIE: All right, Jessie Mae.

JESSIE MAE: And she should realize that. Did you tell your mama what we were discussing in the car?

LUDIE: No. We can talk it all over driving back to Houston.

JESSIE MAE: I think we should have it out right here. I'd like everything understood right now.

[JESSIE MAE *opens her purse and takes out a piece of paper.*]

I've gotten everything written down. Do you want to read it or do you want me to read it to you, Mother Watts?

MRS. WATTS: What is it, Jessie Mae?

JESSIE MAE: It's a few rules and regulations that are necessary to my peace of mind. And I think to Ludie's. Ludie says you may have a few of your own to add and that may be and I'm perfectly willin' to listen if you do . . . First of all, I'd like to ask you a question.

MRS. WATTS: Yes, ma'am.

JESSIE MAE: Just what possessed you to run away? Didn't you know you'd be caught and have to come back?

MRS. WATTS: I had to come, Jessie Mae. Twenty years is a long time.

JESSIE MAE: But what if you had died from the excitement! Didn't you know you could have died?

MRS. WATTS: I knew.

JESSIE MAE: And you didn't care?

MRS. WATTS [*with great dignity*]: I had to come, Jessie Mae.

JESSIE MAE: Well, I hope it's out of your system now.

MRS. WATTS: It is. I've had my trip. That's more than enough to keep me happy the rest of my life.

JESSIE MAE: Well, I'm glad to hear that. That's the first thing on my list.

[*She reads from list.*]

Number one. There'll be no more running away.

MRS. WATTS: There'll be no more running away.

JESSIE MAE: Good.

[*She takes the list up again.*]

Number two. No more hymn singing when I'm in the apartment. When I'm gone, you can sing your lungs out. Agreed?

MRS. WATTS: Agreed.

JESSIE MAE: Number three—

LUDIE [*interrupting*]: Jessie Mae, can't this wait till we get home?

JESSIE MAE: Now, honey, we agreed that I'm going to handle this!

[*She goes back to the list.*]

No more pouting. When I ask a question, I'd like an answer. Otherwise I'll consider it's pouting.

MRS. WATTS: All right.

JESSIE MAE: Fourth. With the condition that your heart is in, I feel you should not run around the apartment when you can walk.

MRS. WATTS: All right, Jessie Mae.

JESSIE MAE: That's all. Is there anything you want to say to me?

MRS. WATTS: No, Jessie Mae.

JESSIE MAE: I might as well tell you now I'm not staying in the house and watching over you anymore. I am joinin' a bridge club and going to town at least twice a week. If you go now, it'll just be your funeral. You understand?

MRS. WATTS: I understand.

JESSIE MAE: All right.

[JESSIE MAE *puts the list away.*]

LUDIE: And, Mama, we also agreed that we're all gonna try our best to get along together. Jessie Mae also realizes that she gets upset sometimes when she shouldn't. Don't you, Jessie Mae?

JESSIE MAE: Uh-huh.

LUDIE: So let's start by trying to have a pleasant ride home.

JESSIE MAE: All rightie. Is there any water around here? I'm thirsty.

LUDIE: I don't think so, Jessie Mae. Mama, is there any water around here?

MRS. WATTS: No. The cistern is gone.

LUDIE [*looking out in the distance*]: When I was a boy, I used to drink in the creek over there, Jessie Mae. We had a cistern, but I always preferred to drink out of the creek. It seemed to me the water always tasted so much better.

JESSIE MAE: Well, you wouldn't catch me drinking out of any creek. I knew a man once that went on a huntin' trip and drank out of a creek and caught something and died.

MRS. WATTS: There's nothin' like cistern water for washin' your hair with. It is the softest water in the world.

[*A bird calls in the distance.*]

That's a redbird.

JESSIE MAE: A what?

MRS. WATTS: A redbird.

JESSIE MAE: Oh. I thought you said that. They all sound alike to me. Well, come on. Let's get going. Do we go back by way of Harrison?

LUDIE: Yes.

JESSIE MAE: Good. Then we can stop at the drugstore. I'm so thirsty I could drink ten Coca-Colas. Are you all ready?

MRS. WATTS: Yes'm.

[JESSIE MAE *looks at her.*]

JESSIE MAE: Where's your purse?

MRS. WATTS: Are you talkin' to me, Jessie Mae?

JESSIE MAE: Who else would I be talkin' to? Since when did Ludie start walkin' around with a pocketbook under his arm?

[MRS. WATTS *looks around.*]

MRS. WATTS: Oh, I guess I left it inside.

JESSIE MAE: Where?

[JESSIE MAE *starts toward the door of the house.*]

MRS. WATTS: I'll get it.

[MRS. WATTS *turns to go into the house.*]

JESSIE MAE: No. I want to go. You'll take all day. Where did you leave it?

MRS. WATTS: In the parlor. Right off the front hall.

JESSIE MAE: All right, I'll get it. You wait here.

[JESSIE MAE *starts into the house.*]

I don't want to be left alone in this ramshackly old house.

[*She goes into the house.*]

LUDIE: Mama.

MRS. WATTS: It's all right, Ludie, son.

[JESSIE MAE *comes back out with the purse.*]

JESSIE MAE: Here's your purse. Now where's the money for that government check?

MRS. WATTS: I haven't cashed it.

JESSIE MAE: Where is it?

MRS. WATTS: It's right inside the purse.

[JESSIE MAE *opens the purse and begins to search again.*]

JESSIE MAE: No. It isn't.

MRS. WATTS: Here let me look.

[JESSIE MAE *hands her the purse and* MRS. WATTS, *too, begins to rummage around. All of a sudden she bursts out laughing.*]

JESSIE MAE: What's the matter with you?

MRS. WATTS: That's a good joke on me.

JESSIE MAE: Well, what's so funny?

MRS. WATTS: I just remembered. I left this purse on the bus last night and caused a man a lot of trouble because I thought the check was in there.

[*She is overcome by laughter again.*]

And do you know that check wasn't in that purse all that time?

JESSIE MAE: Where was it?

MRS. WATTS: Right here.

[*She reaches inside her dress and takes it out.*]

Been here since yesterday afternoon.

[JESSIE MAE *reaches for the check.*]

JESSIE MAE: Give it to me before you go and lose it again.

MRS. WATTS: I won't lose it.

JESSIE MAE: Now don't start that business again. Just give it to me—

LUDIE [*interrupting angrily*]: Jessie Mae.

JESSIE MAE: Well, I'm not going to—

LUDIE: We're going to stop this wrangling once and for all. You've given me your word, and I expect you to keep your word. We have to live together, and we're going to live together in peace.

MRS. WATTS: It's all right, Ludie.

[*She gives the check to* JESSIE MAE.]

Let Jessie Mae take care of the check.

[JESSIE MAE *accepts the check. She looks at it for a moment and then grabs* MRS. WATTS'*s purse. She opens it and puts the check inside.*]

JESSIE MAE: Oh, here. You keep the check. But don't go and lose it before you get home.

[*She puts the purse back in* MRS. WATTS'*s hand. She starts offstage.*]

Well, come on. Let's go.

[*She leaves.* LUDIE *goes to his mother.*]

LUDIE: Mama, if I get a raise you won't—
MRS. WATTS: It's all right, Ludie. I've had my trip. You go ahead. I'll be right there.

[LUDIE *starts out.* MRS. WATTS *points up in the sky.*]

Look, isn't that a scissortail?
LUDIE: I don't know. I didn't get to see it if it was. They fly so fast.

[LUDIE *takes one last look at the house.*]

The house used to look so big.

[*He goes out.* MRS. WATTS *stands for a moment, looking at the sky. She begins to walk. She pauses for a moment, taking one last look at the house.*]

MRS. WATTS [*speaking quietly*]: Good-bye, Bountiful, good-bye.

[MRS. WATTS *looks at the house. The redbird is heard. She moves closer to the house. The hymn is heard a capella very softly, then a little louder.* MRS. WATTS *moves off. She pauses to put her hand on the fence post and then exits. The lights and sound fade.*]

THE YOUNG MAN
FROM ATLANTA

For Lillian

PRODUCTION HISTORY

The Young Man from Atlanta was presented by the Signature Theatre Company (James Houghton, artistic director; Thomas C. Proehl, managing director; Elliot Fox, associate director) in New York City, on January 27, 1995. It was directed by Peter Masterson; the set design was by E. David Cosier; the costume design was by Teresa Snider-Stein and Jonathan Green; the lighting design was by Jeffrey S. Koger; the production stage manager was Dean Gray and the assistant stage manager was Casey A. Rafter.

Will Kidder	Ralph Waite
Tom Jackson	Devon Abner
Miss Lacey	Christina Burz
Ted Cleveland Jr.	Seth Jones
Clara	Frances Foster
Lily Dale Kidder	Carlin Glynn
Pete Davenport	James Pritchett
Carson	Michael Lewis
Etta Doris Meneffree	Beatrice Winde

CHARACTERS

Will Kidder
Tom Jackson
Miss Lacey
Ted Cleveland Jr.
Clara
Lily Dale Kidder
Pete Davenport
Carson
Etta Doris Meneffree

SCENE 1

[*Spring 1950, Houston, Texas. The lights are brought up on the office at the Sunshine Southern Wholesale Grocery. It is a fairly large, comfortable office.* WILL KIDDER, *sixty-four, a hearty, burly man with lots of vitality who has worked for this same firm since his early twenties, is at his desk, with a telephone nearby, and is looking at a set of house plans.* TOM JACKSON, *thirty-five, a colleague and close friend, comes in.*]

TOM: Good morning, Will.

WILL: Good morning, Tom. [*Indicating the house plans*] I was about to put these away now that we've moved into the house. It's a beauty, if I do say so myself. Of course, it cost me a fortune, you know. But shoot, I think it's worth every penny.

TOM: What did it end up costing?

WILL: I haven't gotten to—gather all the final figures. But I'd guess well over two hundred thousand. But it's worth it. There is no finer house in Houston. We have the best of everything.

[*Pause.*]

Excuse me, fellow. I got a little short of breath there for a moment.

TOM: You all right, Will?

WILL: Couldn't be better. I just think I overdid a little this week. I was determined to get everything in place.

[*Pause.*]

Truth is, I have a slight heart condition. Nothing serious, the doctor said. I just have to use common sense and not overdo, the doctor said.

TOM: When did you find this out?

WILL: Yesterday. I wanted to get more life insurance, so I had to go to a doctor for a physical, and when the insurance company read his report, they said it was nothing serious, but I'd have to come back in six months for another examination before they could issue the extra insurance.

TOM: Do you have a good doctor?

WILL: Shoot. The best doctor in Houston. Son, I only go to the best. I learned that lesson a long time ago. You get what you pay for.

TOM: I'm sure that's right.

[*He looks at the house plans.*]

It's none of my business, Will, but I was saying to my wife last night, "Why in this world does he want a big house like that now that there is only two of you?"

WILL: Because I want the best. The biggest and the best. I always have. Since I was a boy. We were dirt-poor after my father died, and I said to myself then, I'm not going to live like this the rest of my life. Will Kidder, I said, you are going from now on to always have the best. And I have. I live in the best country in the world. I live in the best city. I have the finest wife a man could have, work for the best whole-sale produce company in the—

TOM: Was.

WILL: Will be again. I have worked here almost forty years, son. I know its strengths. All of them. We have the best products in the city of Houston, and those we don't have we just have to aggressively compete for. I'm a competitor, son. A born competitor. Nothing fires me up like competition.

[*Pause.*]

My brother, may his soul rest in peace, wasn't. He didn't have a competitive bone in his body. All he ever thought about was where his next drink of whiskey was coming from. I said to my son, "Bill, stay away from whiskey. Whiskey will ruin your life." Bill, I'm happy to say, took my advice.

[*He takes a picture of a young man in his late twenties off his desk.*]

This is my son.

[TOM *takes the photograph and looks at it.*]

My wife had this made for me yesterday.

TOM: A fine-lookin' fellow.

WILL [*taking the photograph back*]: Yes. Never met him, did you?

TOM: No.

WILL [*indicating signed letters*]: Here, you take care of this.

[TOM *takes the letters.*]

It doesn't seem possible he's not here any longer. He was a fine young man. One of the best. We weren't anything at all alike, you know.

TOM: No?

WILL: No, nothing. I'm crazy about sports. He never cared for them. Not that he was artistic like his mother. He wasn't. He had a fine math mind. He was a whiz at math. And he loved school. He was never happier than when he was studying. I thought he was going to stay in college forever. Cost me a fortune. And then the war came along. He was twenty-nine and he volunteered first thing. Couldn't wait to be drafted. Volunteered for the air force. He was a bombardier. Came home without a scratch. Made I don't know how many bombing raids and didn't even get a scratch. I thought, my boy has a charmed life for sure. When the war was over, I wanted to bring him here in the business, but he would have none of it. He got a job in Atlanta. "Why Atlanta?" I said. "You were born and raised in Houston, Texas, the finest city in the whole of the world." I never could figure out exactly what his job was. I don't think he used any of his math skills as far as I could tell. He traveled a lot. He was on a trip for his company that day . . .

[*Pause.*]

I still can't believe it.

TOM: Don't go over all that now if it upsets you.

WILL: No. It does me good to talk about it. I can't talk to my wife about it.

[*Pause.*]

He was in Florida for his company and he stopped at this lake to go for a swim. He couldn't swim. Never learned, and I never remember hearing of him going swimming before. Anyway, that's what he did this day. The man that owned the lake was there alone, and he said it never occurred to him to ask him if he could swim. He said he went into the bathhouse and changed his clothes and came out and waved to him as he walked into the lake. He said he just kept walking until he was out of sight. The man got concerned when he couldn't see him any longer and he yelled to him, and when he got no answer, he got his boat and rowed out to where he had last seen him and found his body. He had drowned. He was thirty-seven—thirty-seven. Drowned. Our only child. I wanted to have more, but my wife had such a difficult time when he was born that we never had any more.

TOM: I wonder why, if he couldn't swim.

WILL: That's what everyone asked. It was the middle of the day. Why in the middle of the day in a lake in Florida out in deep, deep water if you can't swim.

[*Pause.*]

Everyone has their theories, and I appreciate their theories, but I'm a realist. I don't need theories. I know what happened. He committed suicide. Why, I don't know.

TOM: Oh, that's terrible.

WILL: I know. I know. I've never told anybody that before. But that's what I think. I always have. I feel close to you, son. I suppose I shouldn't be saying these things even to you. But I have no one else I feel I can confide in.

TOM: Did he leave children?

WILL: No. He never married. If he even went with a girl, we never knew about it. I've never told my wife what I thought happened. We never discuss that part of it. We talk about how much we miss him and what a fine man he was and what a considerate son, and he was certainly that. A fine and considerate son. My wife has become extremely religious since his death. She was always interested in religion, but now that's all she thinks about. God this and God that.

TOM: Was your son religious?

WILL: No more than I am. I can take it or leave it. He joined the Episcopal church as a young man. Your job was the one I hoped would interest him here in the company, but it didn't.

[MISS LACEY *comes in. She is Will's secretary.*]

MISS LACEY: Excuse me, Mr. Kidder. There is a call for you.

WILL: Who is it from?

MISS LACEY: That same young man.

WILL: Tell him I'm not here.

MISS LACEY: He'll want to know when you'll be here. He always does.

WILL: Say you don't know.

MISS LACEY: Yes, sir.

[*She goes.*]

WILL: That young man was my son's roommate in Atlanta. He was ten years younger than my son. He came here for the funeral and stayed at our house in Bill's old room. He told my wife that our son had become very religious in the year before his death and that every morning you could hear him praying all over their rooming house. I didn't believe it then and I don't believe it now. Sam Curtis, my oldest friend, came to me and said he thought he was a phony and he was making the whole thing up to get money out of us. I said, "Then get rid of him. Get him out of the house." And he did. Right after the funeral. During the funeral he got hysterical and cried more than my wife. She was comforting him and he was comforting her. He calls once a week to talk to me. God knows what he wants. Money, I suppose. Although he tells my secretary he just wants to stay in touch with Bill's dad. Anyway, that's why I'm glad we're leaving the old house where Bill was raised and going into this brand-new house. Even though it's taking all my cash . . .

[*Pause.*]

Yes, my wife has gotten very religious. She reads the Bible constantly. She was always interested in music, composing and playing the piano, until this happened, and now, she won't go near her music or the piano.

[MISS LACEY *comes back in.*]

MISS LACEY: The young man left his telephone number and asked if you would call him at your convenience.

[*She gives him the number on a slip of paper. She goes. He rolls the paper up and throws it in the wastebasket.*]

WILL: He's nervy. I'll say that. He wrote my wife after he left, but I found one of the letters, all about Bill and God, and I told her not to answer.

Maybe next time he calls I'll tell him just to keep the hell away from us.

TOM: Maybe you should tell him now.

WILL: No. I'll wait until he calls again. Maybe he'll at last get the message and not call again.

[*Pause. He reaches in the wastebasket and gets the paper with the phone number out and looks at it.*]

My God. This isn't an Atlanta number. This is a Houston number—Lehigh–six–six thousand. Lehigh–six–six thousand. That's the downtown YMCA. I work out there. My God. I'd better tell him to stay away.

[*He dials the number.*]

Yes. Randy Carter. R-A-N-D-Y—Randy—Carter.
[*To* TOM] I think his name is Randolph, but he always says, "I'm Randy Carter."
[*Into phone*] Yes? . . . Oh. . . . No. No message.

[*He hangs up the phone.*]

He's not there.

[*Pause.*]

My wife's stepfather is living with us. His wife, my wife's mother, has been dead a number of years and he's all alone. His people are all back in Atlanta, Georgia. What's left of them. He moved to Houston when he was a young man of twenty. He married my wife's mother when my wife was only ten, so he is the only father she's ever known. Pete, that's his name. Pete Davenport. I said, "Pete, you wouldn't be kin to this roommate of Bill's back in Atlanta?" "No," he said, "all my close relatives that I know of are dead." "Well," I said, "maybe he's not such a close one. One that you've never heard of." "No," he said, "I don't think so. I don't think he looks like anyone I knew or was kin to me in Atlanta, Georgia."

[*Pause.*]

I don't know why I'm telling you all this. I don't have anyone else I can confide in, and I feel like you're my son in many ways.

TOM: Thank you. I appreciate that.

WILL: Of course you'll never mention any of this to anyone else in the company.

TOM: Oh, no. I won't say a word. You can trust me.

WILL: I know I can. How's your wife and children?

TOM: Fine. Just fine.

WILL: Lovely family you have, son. Be glad you have more than one child. It is very, very difficult when you lose your only child.

TOM: I know that it must be.

WILL: My wife's brother lost his second son in an air raid over Germany, and of course they grieved, but then they have two more sons to think about and help them carry on—well—I hope this new house will help us get away from a lot of memories. To celebrate the new house, I'm buying my wife a new car.

TOM: Will, we lost three more accounts today. Three of our largest. Carnation Milk is one, and I understand it has been with us since the beginning of the company.

WILL: When did you find this out?

TOM: I just heard it.

WILL: Who told you?

TOM: Mister Cleveland Junior. He's in his office today.

WILL: Why in the hell didn't he tell me?

TOM: I don't know, sir. Please don't say I told you.

WILL: No.

TOM: I'm sure he'll tell you.

WILL: I'm sure. Well, it doesn't worry me at all.

TOM: Come on, Will.

WILL: We went through the Depression with flying colors, when the rest of Houston was on its knees. Begging for mercy—not us. Not us. We were prospering.

[TED CLEVELAND JR., *forty-four, enters.*]

TED: Hello, Will.

WILL: Hello, Ted. I was just telling Tom how we weathered the Depression with flying colors. Your dad used to say to me, "Nothing ever gets you down, does it?" No, sir. Nothing. Not Roosevelt. Not the New Deal. Not bureaucrats, nothing. I remember the time, Ted, I told your dad I had decided to vote the Republican ticket for the first time and that if he didn't want to see this country ruined, he'd better do the same. "I can't do that, Will," he said. "My granddaddy was a captain in the Confederate army, my mama heads the U.D.C. here in Houston." "Hell," I said. "What was that war all about? States' rights—and who is for states' rights? The Republicans or the Democrats?" Of course, he couldn't argue with that. So a day later he called me into his office and said, "You've converted me. I'm voting Republican." And he did. Your father was a hell of a man, Ted. They don't make them like that anymore.

TED: No, they sure don't.

[*Pause.*]

Will you excuse us, Tom?

TOM: Sure.

[TOM *puts the letters on Will's desk.*]

WILL: No, you look into this.

[TOM *takes the letters and leaves.*]

TED: How is your wife, Will?

WILL: Pretty fair. Considering everything.

TED: Terrible about your son. I suppose she's gradually getting over it. Of course, I don't suppose you ever really get over such things. Not a son. Not an only son.

WILL: It's not easy. How are your wife and children?

TED: They're all well, thank you. Spend too much money, but otherwise I can't complain. How do you like Tom?

WILL: He's a fine young man.

TED: I think so.

WILL: I hired him, you know. I trained him.

TED: Yes, I'm aware of that.

[*Pause.*]

The company is going through a bad patch, Will. We've just lost three more accounts. Including Carnation.

WILL: You don't say. When did you hear this?

TED: Yesterday.

WILL: I wish you would have told me this right away. You know, I've handled the Carnation account from its beginning with the company. They respect me over there. We've done business together now for over thirty years. And if I do say so myself . . .

TED: May I be frank, Will?

WILL: Yes, sir.

TED: You're the reason they're giving for leaving us.

WILL: Me?

TED: Yes. You. They feel you're not "with it" any longer, as they say.

WILL: Who says? Not Cochran Judd. Why, he and I—

TED: No, not Cochran Judd. He's been fired.

WILL: My God. When?

TED: As of yesterday. There have been a lot of replacements there, I believe. It's a new age, Will. My father wouldn't recognize business as it's done today. Very competitive.

WILL: Shoot. That doesn't scare me. I thrive on competition, Ted. When I started with this company, when your dad and I were young men, that's what made us the success we became. Our competitive spirit. Your dad said to me one day, "Will, I've always thought of myself as a competitive man, but you're the most competitive man I've ever known or seen. The most." That is what he said. And he called me into his office just before he died and he said, "Will, I'm going to die soon, I know, but I'm going with peace of mind knowing you are here to help my son run the company. The company we built together, Will."

[*Pause.*]

TED: It's a different ball game, Will. What worked forty years ago, or twenty, or ten, doesn't work anymore. I'm going to have to replace you, Will. You'll have three months' notice beginning today.

WILL: Ted.

TED: My hands are tied, Will. We have to change our ways of doing business or we'll go under. We're not competing any longer, Will.

WILL: What kind of changes are you talking about? I can change . . .

TED: I don't think so, Will. We need younger men in charge here.

WILL: Younger men?

TED: Yes. In their twenties, thirties . . .

WILL: Younger men?

TED: Yes, I'm sorry.

[TED *sees the house plans. He points to them.*]

What are these?

WILL: This is the house I built.

TED: Oh, yes. I rode by there the other night to take a look at it. Very handsome.

WILL: Thank you.

[TED *sees Bill's picture.*]

TED: And this is your son?

WILL: Yes.

TED: Very tragic. I know it was quite a blow.

WILL: Yes, sir. It was.

[TED *gets up.*]

TED: Well, thank you for being so understanding. I'm sure you know how much I appreciate all you have done for the company through the years.

WILL: Thank you.

[TED *starts out of the room.*]

Ted.

TED: Yes?

WILL: I always thought about starting my own company, but I would never do it out of loyalty to your father, but now, I may be starting my own company.

TED: Oh. Well, I wish you luck. You certainly know what you'll be facing. Do you have enough capital to get going?

WILL: I'll start in a very small way.

TED: Well, good luck to you, Will.

WILL: Thanks.

TED: I suppose under these circumstances you'll be leaving the company right away.

WILL: Yes, sir.

TED: Good luck to you again.

[TED *goes.* WILL *goes to the phone.*]

WILL [*into the phone*]: Dawson Motor Company. This is Will Kidder. I'm going to have to cancel the order on the car.

[*Pause.*]

I understand, and I'm sorry. I am hoping I can have my deposit back. . . . Under the circumstances. . . . I see. I understand. . . . No. I understand.

[*He hangs up the phone. He picks it up again.*]

Miss Lacey. Ask Tom to come in. Thank you.

[*He opens the drawer of his desk and begins to go through its contents, discarding items into the wastebasket.* TOM *comes in.*]

Sit down, son. My life is just about to change. And being an optimist, I think for the better. I'm going to try and start my own company. In a modest way for now.

TOM: Oh.

WILL: It's something I've wanted to do for a long time, but I wouldn't out of loyalty to this company, but now . . .

[*Pause.*]

I've been fired. Replaced by younger men.

TOM: I'm sorry.

WILL: I won't lie to you. It's quite a blow to my pride. But never mind. I've had worse blows than this, and on I'll go. I'll be honest with you. It's come at a bad time. I've put a lot of my cash in the new house.

TOM: But you've savings, I'm sure . . .

WILL: Not much. My savings went into the house. But I have friends in every bank in Houston. I know they'll help me get started. They'll stand by me until I'm on my feet once again. I'm going slow, you know, all I need is a hundred thousand, two hundred thousand—

[*Pause.*]

I hope after I've gotten started that you'll join me. I wouldn't ask you to come aboard just now because I know you have responsibilities, a wife and children, but once I get going, I'm coming back to you, and I hope—

[*Pause.*]

Do you know who they've hired to take my place?
TOM: Yes, I do.
WILL: Who is it? Anyone I know?
TOM: Yes. It's me, Will.

[*Pause.*]

I feel terrible about it, but Ted explained that no matter what I did . . .
WILL: I understand, son. Well, good luck to you.
TOM: Thank you.
WILL: Excuse me, now. I have to make a phone call about my financing.
TOM: Sure.

[TOM *goes.* WILL *picks up the phone and dials.*]

WILL: Hello. Yes, sir. This is Will Kidder. . . . Will Kidder. I want to come in and talk to you about a proposition that I think you'll find very interesting. . . . Will Kidder. K-I-D-D-E-R. . . . Yes. Kidder. . . .

[*He continues talking on as the lights fade.*]

SCENE 2

[*The next evening. The lights are brought up on a section of the den in the new house of the Kidders.* WILL *is alone, sitting on the couch. As lights rise,* CLARA *enters with coffee service followed by* LILY DALE KIDDER *and* PETE DAVENPORT.]

LILY DALE: Thank you, Clara.
CLARA: You're welcome.

[CLARA *exits.*]

LILY DALE: It was a lovely supper, wasn't it? I tell you, I believe Clara is the best cook we've ever had. During the war, you know, Mrs. Roosevelt got all the maids in Houston to join the Disappointment Club.

PETE: Did she? I never heard about that.

LILY DALE: You didn't? It was just awful. A maid would say they were going to work for you. You would arrange the hours and the salary and she would be so nice and polite. Then the day she was supposed to start work, she wouldn't show up, and that meant she was a member of the Disappointment Club whose purpose was to disappoint white people.

WILL: And you think Mrs. Roosevelt was behind that?

LILY DALE: I know she was. Everybody in Houston knows she was. She just hated the South, you know. She took out all her personal unhappiness on the South.

WILL: Shoot. Somebody sold you a bill of goods, Lily Dale. I never cared much for either of the Roosevelts, as you know, but I don't think Mrs. Roosevelt organized the maids in Houston into anything.

LILY DALE: Well, she did.

WILL: All right. She did.

[*Pause.*]

LILY DALE: Daddy?

WILL: What?

LILY DALE: Why are you so cross?

WILL: I don't mean to be cross. I'm tired, I guess. I'm sorry.

LILY DALE: That's all right, Daddy. I guess you have a right to be tired as hard as you work. He's been so good to me all my life, Pete. Anything I ever wanted Will got for me.

PETE: I know that.

LILY DALE: When is my new car going to be here, Daddy?

WILL: That may have to wait a while now, Lily Dale. The house and the furnishings just cost more than I figured. I want to get them all paid for before I take on any more debts.

LILY DALE: The house is so beautiful, Will.

[*Pause.*]

I wish Bill could have seen it.

[*Pause.*]

I miss Bill so much, Daddy.

WILL: I know.

LILY DALE: Not that we saw much of him these last years, but it was just knowing you could call him on the phone when you wanted to. Or that he'd be with us at Christmas. The minute he'd come home for Christmas he'd ask me what new pieces I had composed, remember? And then he'd say play it for me. I'd say, "You haven't called your daddy at the office," and he'd say, "Time enough for that. I want to hear your new pieces right this very minute."

[*Pause.*]

I don't compose anymore, Pete.

PETE: I know.

LILY DALE: I haven't gone near the piano since Bill died. That all seems too frivolous to me now. Vanity. Vanity. Things of this world. Vanity. Vanity.

[WILL *gets up.*]

WILL: I'm tired. I'm going to bed. Glad to have you here with us, Pete.

PETE: Thank you. Nice to be here.

[WILL *starts out of the room and then pauses.*]

WILL: Lily Dale, that roommate Bill had back in Atlanta is here in Houston.

LILY DALE: Oh?

WILL: He called the office today. Has he called here?

LILY DALE: No.

WILL: If he does, let him know we want nothing to do with him.

LILY DALE: You told me that before, Daddy. I still don't understand what happened to turn you so against him. You seemed to like him so much at first. You seem . . .

WILL: I have my reasons, Lily Dale.

LILY DALE: I'm sure you do.

WILL: Good night.

LILY DALE: Good night.

PETE: Good night.

[WILL *goes*.]

LILY DALE: I don't know why he's turned against him. Do you?
PETE: No.
LILY DALE: What did you think of him, Pete?
PETE: I didn't say more than two words to him, Lily Dale, the whole time he was here.
LILY DALE: I don't care what Daddy says. I think he is a very sweet boy. I can't tell you what it meant to me when he told me how religious Bill had become. Why, he said every morning you could hear him pray all over the boardinghouse. He said they were the most beautiful prayers he had ever heard. He said everybody in the boardinghouse just stopped whatever they were doing to listen to him pray.

[*Pause.*]

Allie Temple committed suicide, I heard today. She took poison.
PETE: She was from Harrison, wasn't she?
LILY DALE: Yes, but she hadn't lived there for years. Her husband, Lawrence, killed himself. I guess it was twenty years ago. He hung himself. Alice was an atheist, you know. I went over to see her a month or so ago and I said, "Alice, my son, Bill, told me the last time he was at home, 'There are no atheists in foxholes.'" "Is that so," she said, very sarcastically. "You aren't really an atheist are you, Alice?" "I am," she said, "confirmed." "My heavens," I told her, "I couldn't ever in this world be an atheist. God has been too good to me." "He certainly has been good to you," she said, again most sarcastically. "Only why did this good God let your son commit suicide?" "What on earth are you talking about," I said. "His death was an accident." "If it was an accident," she said, "what was he doing in a lake over his head, when he couldn't swim?" "It was a hot day," I said, "that's why he went for a swim." "And how many swims had he ever gone to before? Ask your God to explain that." And she upset me so, Pete, that I couldn't stop trembling and my heart started racing so, I thought I would have a heart attack. And I just had to call that sweet roommate of his in Atlanta, even though Daddy had told me never to, and I told him exactly what Alice had told me. He said there was not a word of truth

in it, and he had talked to him from Florida the night before on the telephone and the whole time they talked about God. So, I felt very relieved after that, and I thanked God, got on my knees and thanked God for sending this sweet friend of Bill's to tell me once again of Bill's faith in God. I could never be an atheist. Could you, Pete?

PETE: No.

LILY DALE: My cousin Willa Thornton is, you know. Least she says she is. She says all the terrible things that have happened to her family make her an atheist. Pete, you do believe in God, don't you?

PETE: Yes, I do.

LILY DALE: I'm glad of that. I wish you'd start going to church with me, Pete.

PETE: Maybe I will one Sunday.

LILY DALE: Will won't go with me to church. He says he believes in God, but he can't stand church. Don't ever tell Will I called that friend of Bill's. I've never done anything in my life I felt Will disapproved of, but this one time I had to disobey him.

[*Pause.*]

Pete, if I tell you something, promise you won't breathe it to another soul?

PETE: I promise.

LILY DALE: Every time I feel blue over missing Bill, I call his friend and I ask him to tell me again about Bill and his prayers and he does so so sweetly. And I've been helping him too, Pete.

PETE: How have you been helping him?

LILY DALE: Loaning him money. Well, not loaning it to him exactly. Although he says that's how he feels about it. You know he's been so blue and depressed since Bill died that he couldn't keep his mind on his job and he got fired, and so I sent him five thousand dollars until he could get himself together, and then . . .

PETE: Is that all you sent him, Lily Dale?

LILY DALE: No, not all.

PETE: How much have you given him, Lily Dale?

LILY DALE: I don't know exactly. I've got it written down somewhere. His mother got sick and needed an operation and I sent him ten thou-

sand for her, and his sister's husband deserted her and she has three
small children and so I sent—

PETE: Lily Dale.

LILY DALE: It's my money, Pete. I prayed about it, and God said that's
what Bill would want me to do, and Randy—that's the name of Bill's
friend—said he was sure it was because he said Bill was going to make
him the beneficiary of his life insurance, and that's another reason he
knew he didn't commit suicide: because he hadn't had time to change
his life insurance making him the beneficiary.

PETE: Lily Dale.

LILY DALE: It's my money, Pete. Will gave me the money every Christmas,
and he always said, "Spend it like you want to," and I never spent any
of it because there was nothing I needed or wanted, and I kept it all
untouched, just in case one day Bill might need something to buy a
house when he got married . . .

[*Pause.*]

Do you know what's troubling Daddy, Pete? He seemed so quiet at
supper. So depressed. It's not like Daddy to be depressed.

PETE: No.

LILY DALE: Do you know what's troubling him?

PETE: Yes, I do.

LILY DALE: What is it, Pete?

PETE: I don't think I can tell you.

LILY DALE: Why can't you tell me, Pete?

PETE: Because I think Will would be mad at me if I did.

LILY DALE: Did he ask you not to tell me?

PETE: Yes.

LILY DALE: Do you think he'll ever tell me?

PETE: I think he will. Yes, I do.

LILY DALE: When?

PETE: At the right time.

LILY DALE: You scare me, Pete. Is it something bad?

PETE: I can't say any more, Lily Dale.

LILY DALE: I won't sleep tonight now for worry. I've got lots to worry
me, Pete.

PETE: I'm sorry.

LILY DALE: I haven't slept hardly a night through since Bill died.

PETE: I'm sure.

LILY DALE: Will just sleeps the whole night through. I know he misses Bill, but it doesn't seem to affect his sleep.

[*Pause.*]

I have another worry now, Pete. I knew Bill's friend was in Houston. He's been out here twice today. He needs a job so badly. I'm praying that Will has a change of heart and finds a job for him at his company. If he knows how Will feels about him, he doesn't let on. He told me he had been calling him. He needs a job and he needs a father; he's hoping Will will be a father to him. He said Bill was like a father to him, gave him advice in all things. He never knew his own father. He died when he was two. I know what that's like, Pete, having lost my own father when I was eight. But I was lucky because Mama married you and you became a wonderful father to me, but, unfortunately, his mother married a man that was a drunkard and he beat him and his sister. I've asked him to visit me here in the afternoons while Will is at work, whenever he gets blue, but you mustn't ever tell Will this, Pete, until God changes his heart, and he will change his heart, that I know, because Will is a good man, a kind man. Don't you think he will change about this, Pete?

PETE: Maybe so. I hope so if that's what you want.

LILY DALE: It's certainly what I want.

[WILL *comes in. He is in his robe and pajamas.*]

Couldn't you sleep?

WILL: No.

LILY DALE: I thought you were sleepy?

WILL: I thought so, too. But I'm not.

LILY DALE: Anything worrying you, Will?

WILL: To tell you the truth, there is. I was going to wait a day or two before telling you this, but I guess I'd better get it over with.

PETE: You want me to leave, Will?

WILL: No, you stay. You know about it anyway. I've been fired, Lily Dale.

LILY DALE: What?

WILL: Fired.

LILY DALE: From the company?

WILL: Yes.

LILY DALE: Why on earth—

WILL: They are replacing me with a younger man. Tom Jackson.

LILY DALE: Tom Jackson. Why, you hired him, trained him.

WILL: I know. I know. He feels terrible about it.

LILY DALE: Will, if he feels so terrible about it, why—

WILL: There's nothing he can do about it. If he didn't take the job, they'd just give it to someone else. They want younger men.

LILY DALE: Who does?

WILL: Ted Cleveland Junior.

LILY DALE: Oh, I think it's scandalous. What will you do, Will?

WILL: I'm going to start my own company if I can get one of the banks to finance me. They told me I could stay on at the company for three months, but I said I wanted to leave right away. I'll spend tomorrow talking to some of my banker friends about a loan.

[*Pause.*]

I hate to ask this, Lily Dale, but I may need some cash. How much do you have left of those Christmas checks I've given you?

LILY DALE: Let's see—

WILL: I'll just need to borrow it back for a month or so.

LILY DALE: Well—and then you have Bill's money that you gave him that you were going to give to me after he died—

WILL: That money was all spent.

LILY DALE: Spent?

WILL: Yes.

LILY DALE: How? Bill never spent money on anything that I knew of. He spent no money on clothes, you gave him his car. He didn't even have an apartment—he lived in a boardinghouse.

WILL: That's perfectly true.

LILY DALE: Then how did he spend it, Will?

WILL: I don't know how he spent it. There was nothing in his room.

LILY DALE: I don't understand it.

WILL: Neither do I. But that's how it is. His life insurance barely paid the funeral expenses. Would you mind going down in the morning and getting your money? I gave you five thousand for fifteen Christmases, so you should have at least seventy-five thousand unless you've spent some of it.

[*Pause.*]

Have you spent any of it?

LILY DALE: Not that I remember.

WILL: Thank God. I'm going to need every nickel I can get until I get this all straightened out, and don't look so upset, honey. I will get it straightened out. We'll be back on our feet before you can turn around good. You know your husband. I always land on my feet.

[*Pause.*]

Well, I feel better now that's off my chest. I think I can sleep now. Are you coming to bed, honey?

LILY DALE: I'll be along later.

[*He goes. There is a pause. She goes to the door to listen to see if he has really gone to his room. When she thinks he has, she turns to* PETE.]

Pete, what am I going to do? Over half that money is gone.

PETE: My God, Lily Dale.

LILY DALE: I don't think there is twenty-five thousand left.

PETE: My God.

LILY DALE: Pete, could you loan me some money?

PETE: All I have, Lily Dale, is the money that's left from the sale of your mama's and my duplex.

LILY DALE: How much is left, Pete?

PETE: Thirty-five thousand.

LILY DALE: Will you give that to me, please, Pete?

PETE: Lily Dale, it's all I have in this world except for my social security. If I should get sick . . .

LILY DALE: I'll find a way to pay you back, Pete. As soon as Will gets on his feet again, he'll give me back the money I've loaned him, and I'll give it to you right away.

[*Pause.*]

Please, Pete.

PETE: Lily Dale—

LILY DALE: Please, Pete. Please—

PETE: All right. I'll get it in the morning.

LILY DALE: Oh, thank you, Pete. Thank you. You've been so good to me all my life and I'm so grateful to you, Pete. I am. I am.

PETE: I know. I know, Lily Dale.

[WILL *comes back in.*]

LILY DALE: Still not sleepy, Will?

WILL: No.

LILY DALE: Would you like me to fix you some hot milk? That might make you sleepy.

WILL: No, thank you.

[*Pause.*]

I might as well come out with it. I'm going to have to ask you to help me, Pete.

PETE: I want to help in any way I can, Will. You know that. I think for one thing I should start paying board and room as long as I stay here.

WILL: Come on, Pete.

PETE: I think I should. I wanted to from the beginning, but Lily Dale said you would never hear of it.

WILL: That's right, and I still won't hear of it. You really hurt me, Pete, even mentioning it.

PETE: I meant no offense, Will.

[*Pause.*]

In what way can I help you, Will?

WILL: How much do you have in savings?

PETE: Well, let's see. Thirty-five thousand dollars, more or less.

WILL: Thirty-five thousand?

PETE: Uh-huh—more or less. That's what I got when I sold the duplex. I have it in savings in case I get sick or—when I die, of course, if it's all still there, I was going to leave it to you and Lily Dale.

[*Pause.*]

Why did you want to know about my savings, Will?

WILL: Pete—

LILY DALE: You want me to go, Will?

WILL: No, you stay here. You might as well hear it, too. I think you know I want to start my own business in a very conservative way. I went to a few banks yesterday to test the waters, and it's clear they are not going to loan me all the money I need. Now, I think you know me well enough that I don't have to tell you that I am a very responsible man.

PETE: You're certainly that, Will.

WILL: I'm competitive, a hard worker—

PETE: All of that, Will.

WILL: But right now I've got my back against the wall. I need, conservatively, to start my own business, three hundred thousand dollars, but I feel sure now the banks won't help out unless I have some money of my own—now, Lily Dale is going to loan me her seventy-five thousand dollars.

LILY DALE: Now, I'm not sure it's seventy-five thousand dollars, Daddy.

WILL: All right. More or less. And Pete, if you could loan me just for a month or so your thirty-five thousand. That would give me a hundred and ten thousand and I could put up the house as security and—

PETE: Well—

WILL: I'd pay you good interest, Pete. I'd give you a note and better interest than you could get anywhere in Houston. I'll pay you back out every first earned dollar and I'd give you an interest in the business besides.

[LILY DALE *begins to cry.*]

What's the matter, Lily Dale?

[*She continues crying.*]

What's the matter?

LILY DALE: You tell him, Pete. I can't bear to tell him.

PETE: Lily Dale, I don't want to get mixed up in this. You better tell him.

LILY DALE: I can't, Pete. I can't—

PETE: All right.

[*Pause.*]

Lily Dale asked me to loan her my thirty-five thousand so you wouldn't find out.

[*Pause.*]

WILL: Find out what?
PETE: You're sure you want me to tell him, Lily Dale?
LILY DALE: Yes. He has to know.
PETE: Well, Lily Dale has given part of the money you gave her—
WILL: Part? How much?
PETE: I don't know how much. How much, Lily Dale?
LILY DALE: Thirty-five thousand dollars, I believe.
WILL: You believe?
LILY DALE: Yes, I believe.
WILL: Who did you give it to?

[*Pause.*]

Was it a loan?
LILY DALE: They say they consider it so, but I didn't give it as a loan.
WILL: I don't understand.
LILY DALE: It was given as a gift. I didn't ask to be paid back.
WILL: Can they pay you back?
LILY DALE: I don't think so. Not right away, anyway.

[*Pause.*]

You told me, Will, the money was mine to do what I wanted to with it. I had saved it, thinking I'll give it to Bill when he married to buy a house, but then he died.
WILL: Who did you give it to?

[*Pause.*]

Do you know who she gave it to, Pete?
PETE: Yes.
WILL: Who?
PETE: I'd rather Lily Dale would tell you.

[LILY DALE *is still crying.*]

WILL: Will you please stop crying, Lily Dale, and tell me who you gave the money to?

[*Pause.*]

Lily Dale—

LILY DALE: That sweet young friend of Bill's.

WILL: Oh, my God. I told you not to go near him. Ever again.

LILY DALE: I know you did.

WILL: What the hell do you mean giving him my money?

LILY DALE: You said it was my money. You said when you gave it to me I could do with it like I wanted to.

WILL: Not to throw it away on bums, I didn't.

LILY DALE: I don't think he's a bum, Will.

WILL: Well, I do. B-U-M—bum. Get it back from him. He's at the YMCA. Call him up and get it back. Tell him if he doesn't give it back, I'll have him arrested. I'm going down there right now and get it from him. I'll break his neck. You lied to me, Lily Dale. You told me you hadn't been near that boy. You lied to me. Goddamn it. Why did you lie to me? Why? Why? Why?

[*Pause.*]

LILY DALE: I don't know. I felt sorry for him. He lost his job because he was so upset over Bill's death and then his mother got sick and needed a serious operation and then his sister had three small children and her husband deserted her.

WILL: Bull.

LILY DALE: That's the truth. That's what he told me.

WILL: Bull. You've been taken for a fool woman. All right. I'm going to sell this goddamn house and use the money in my business. We'll live in a tourist court. I'm firing Clara tomorrow. You can do the housework for a change. I'm sick of working myself to death for you to give my good money to deadbeats.

[WILL *goes.*]

LILY DALE: Oh, Pete. Go to him. He's all upset. Calm him down. Go to him, Pete.

PETE: Maybe you should go to him, Lily Dale.

LILY DALE: No, he doesn't want to see me. He hates me now. Go to him, Pete. Please.

[PETE *goes.* LILY DALE *puts her head in her hands. She is trying to control her crying.* PETE *comes back in.*]

PETE: Call his doctor, Lily Dale. He thinks it's his heart.
LILY DALE: My God, my God.

[*She goes to the phone as the lights fade.*]

SCENE 3

[*The lights are brought up on the study. It is a week later.* CLARA, *the maid, is there dusting.* LILY DALE *enters.*]

LILY DALE: Oh, hello, Clara.
CLARA: That young man from Atlanta says he was a friend of your son's came by again this morning looking for you.
LILY DALE: What did you tell him?
CLARA: I told him you weren't home. He called twice before he came over.
LILY DALE: Oh, Clara. I'm a nervous wreck. Everything is just so awful.
CLARA: Where is your Christian faith?
LILY DALE: I know. I know. Thank you for reminding me. And I need all the Christian faith I can muster. Clara, let me tell you, I haven't slept for five nights. I am a nervous wreck. I have been deceived. I have been so deceived it has just broken my heart.
CLARA: Who deceived you, darling?
LILY DALE: That young man. Bill's friend from Atlanta.
CLARA: How did he deceive you, darling?
LILY DALE: In all ways. You see, I had some money that Will gave me over a number of Christmases, and after Bill died, this young man came for the funeral and he told me Bill had become very religious and that they were devoted to each other and that Bill was going to make him the beneficiary in his will and he . . .

[*She begins to cry.*]

CLARA: Now, now.

LILY DALE: I feel so betrayed, so hurt, so humiliated. Dear God, why? Why?

[*Pause.*]

Anyway, he said he was so upset over Bill's death he couldn't work, and I sent him money to help out until he could find work, and then he said he had a sick mother who needed an operation and a sister—

[*She cries again.*]

Oh, it's just awful, Clara. It's just awful.

CLARA: Now, now.

LILY DALE: And I gave him money, and then Will lost his job and said he needed to borrow that money he had given me and I went to my stepfather to ask him to loan me money to make up for the money I had given Bill's friend and before my stepfather could get me the money Will asked if he could borrow the money from my stepfather so I had to tell him what I'd done with my money, and he was furious of course and he had his heart attack and he almost died.

CLARA: Well, he didn't die, now. So you can thank God for that.

LILY DALE: I know. I know, and I am thankful for that. But it isn't bad enough I deceived Will and gave the money without telling him, although it was my money to do with like I wanted, he always said.

CLARA: Well, then.

LILY DALE: But then yesterday a distant relative of Pete's from Atlanta showed up here named Carson and Pete asked Carson if he had known Bill and his friend in Atlanta and he said he had, and he said that Bill was a fine fellow, but he didn't care much for his friend, who he had known all his life. And Pete asked him how Bill's friend's sick mother was and he said he had no mother living, that he had no family at all since he was an only child, and Pete asked him about Bill being religious and he said it was the first he had heard of it, that he had a room in the boardinghouse, too, and that if he ever prayed it was to himself and he hadn't heard a single prayer from Bill the whole time he lived there. Oh, Clara.

CLARA: Now, now.

LILY DALE: Will is not half speaking to me now. I don't know what's going to become of us, Clara. Pete tells me we are in very bad shape financially. Will can't work now even if he wanted to, and we have no money except what I have left from my Christmas gifts.

CLARA: God is going to take care of you.

LILY DALE: You think so?

CLARA: He takes care of me. I have lots to worry me, too, you know. Some mornings I just feel like not getting out of bed, but I say, "Clara, get on up. God is gonna take care of you." And just look around you, you've got this beautiful brand-new house.

LILY DALE: Which is paid for. Thank God. But Pete tells me the furniture is not. I said, "Daddy, I don't need new furniture, let's make do with the furniture we have in our old house." "No," he said, "I want everything new here."

[PETE *comes in with* CARSON, *his relative.*]

PETE: Lily Dale, this is my great-nephew, Carson.

LILY DALE: Hello, Carson. Welcome to Houston.

CARSON: Thank you.

PETE: Carson brought along a picture of my sister, who was his grandmother. I wouldn't have recognized her. She married a Mister Stewart. She had four children including Carson's mother.

LILY DALE: Oh? Sit down, Carson.

PETE: Carson says they're all dead except his older sister Vivian and his youngest sister, Susette.

CARSON: Vivian never married. Susette married and has six children. Two of them not quite right. It's a real burden for her.

LILY DALE: My goodness. This is Clara, Carson. She works here for us.

CLARA: How do you do.

CARSON: How do you do.

CLARA: I have a sister who has a child that has fits. She can't leave the house because she has to put every living minute into watching that child.

LILY DALE: Pete says you knew Bill?

CARSON: Oh, yes. He was a fine fellow.

LILY DALE: He certainly was that.

CARSON: I knew his roommate, too. I didn't think too much of him.

LILY DALE: No?

CARSON: No. A big talker.

LILY DALE: I see.

CARSON: Always bragging.

LILY DALE: Where did he work?

CARSON: He never worked as far as I know.

[WILL *comes in. He is in his pajamas and robe.*]

LILY DALE: Do you think you ought to be out of bed, Will?

WILL: If I didn't think so, I wouldn't be.

PETE: Will, this is my great-nephew, Carson.

WILL: Pleased to know you, Carson.

[*Pause.*]

How do you like Houston?

CARSON: Fine, what little I've seen of it.

WILL: Where are you staying?

CARSON: At the YMCA.

WILL: Ah, yes.

LILY DALE: Clara, did you ever hear of the maids organizing Disappointment Clubs in Houston during the war?

CLARA: No, ma'am. I sure didn't.

LILY DALE: Maybe you were right, Will.

WILL: I know I'm right about Mrs. Roosevelt.

[*The doorbell rings.*]

CLARA: Excuse me.

[*She goes to the front door.*]

CARSON: What are Disappointment Clubs?

LILY DALE: Well, I was always told that Mrs. Roosevelt—

[TOM JACKSON *comes in. He has a bouquet of flowers.*]

Well, hello, Tom. Will, Tom is here.

WILL: Hello, Tom.

TOM: Hello, young man. I thought I'd find you in bed.

WILL: I just got up. I get tired of the bed, Tom.

TOM: I brought these flowers for you.

WILL: Thank you, Tom.

[WILL *takes the flowers from* TOM.]

LILY DALE: Aren't they pretty. [*Calling*] Clara!
WILL: This is my stepfather-in-law, Tom. Pete Davenport.
TOM: How do you do.

[TOM *and* PETE *shake hands.*]

WILL: And what's your name, young man?
CARSON: Carson.
TOM: Hello, Carson. Tom Jackson.

[TOM *and* CARSON *shake hands.*]

PETE: He's my great-nephew. He's just come here from Atlanta. He's
    looking for a job. You don't know of a job, do you?
TOM: Not right offhand.
WILL: Tom works at my old company.
LILY DALE: I don't see how they had the heart to do that to Will, Tom.
    As hard as he worked for that company through the years.
WILL: Let's change the subject, Lily Dale. Tom had nothing to do
    with it.
LILY DALE: I know he didn't have anything to do with it, Daddy. Carson,
    my husband worked for a company for—
WILL: Let's change the subject, Lily Dale. The doctor says I'm not sup-
    posed to dwell on all of that. It's not good for me.
LILY DALE: All right, Will, I'm sorry.

[CLARA *comes in.*]

CLARA: You wanted me.
LILY DALE: Yes. Please take those pretty flowers and put them in water
    and a vase.

[CLARA *takes them.*]

CLARA: They are pretty. I called my friend Lucille and I asked her if she
    even knew of them Disappointment Clubs. She said she'd heard of
    them but wouldn't have anything to do with them.
LILY DALE: See, Will? Ask your friend if Mrs. Roosevelt was behind
    it all.

CLARA: Yes, ma'am.

[CLARA *takes the flowers and goes.*]

WILL: I think the banks in Houston are all running Disappointment Clubs. I've been doing business with almost every bank in Houston in one way or another for forty years. When I went to see them yesterday about starting my own business, they looked at me like they never heard of me.

TOM: That happens. Then one day you go in and talk to someone else and it'll be a different story.

WILL: Anyway, I can't work for a while.

TOM: When you get stronger, I wish you'd come down to the company. I was talking to Ted last night. He thinks he may be able to find something for you to do, less responsibility, I suppose.

WILL: No, Tom. I'll never go back there. I was very hurt by that, you know.

TOM: I know you were, and I don't blame you.

CARSON: Do you still work, Uncle Pete?

PETE: No, son, I retired a long time ago. I was with the Southern Pacific. Engineer.

CARSON: My daddy was an engineer.

PETE: Is that right.

CARSON: He drank, though, and they fired him. Mama says he never left the house—that she didn't pray he wouldn't have a wreck because of his drinking.

[*The doorbell rings.*]

PETE: You better not drink and run engines. I never drank in my life. I worked since I was fourteen until I retired.

CARSON: Mama says Grandma says you were always a hard worker. When was the last time you were in Atlanta, Uncle Pete?

PETE: Thirty years, I guess.

CARSON: You wouldn't know it now.

PETE: I guess not.

[CLARA *enters.*]

CLARA: That young man is here again.

WILL: What young man?

CLARA: Mr. Bill's roommate from Atlanta.

LILY DALE: Tell him we're not here.

CLARA: He can see you all in here.

LILY DALE: Tell him we're busy.

WILL: Let me tell him.

[*He starts up.*]

LILY DALE: Now, Daddy. You must not get excited. Just keep calm. Clara, tell him we can't see him and not to come anymore.

CARSON: Is that Bill's old roommate? He's bad news.

[LILY DALE *begins to cry. She starts out of the room.*]

LILY DALE: Excuse me.

[LILY DALE *goes.*]

CARSON: Did I say something to upset somebody?

WILL: No. Don't worry about it.

CARSON: I was telling Great Uncle Pete that he is nothing but a four flusher.

PETE: Let's change the subject, son.

CARSON: Sure. Whatever you say.

TOM: Ted said he'd like to come by and see you, but he wasn't sure you'd want him to.

WILL: I'd just as soon he'd not come.

TOM: He said he sent you a get well card.

WILL: I got it.

[*Pause.*]

TOM: Well, I guess I'd better be on my way. I don't want to overtire you. I hope you'll be feeling better soon, Will.

WILL: Thank you.

[WILL *gets up.*]

TOM: Don't get up, Will. I can find my way out. Take care of yourself, Will. Tell Lily Dale good-bye for me, Will.

[*He turns to* PETE *and* CARSON.]

Nice to have met you both.

CARSON: Same here.

PETE: Nice to have met you, sir.

[TOM *goes*.]

WILL: He was the one who took my job. I brought him into the company and trained him, and they gave him my job. I didn't think I felt any hard feelings toward him, but I do. God help me. I do. I gave my life for that company, you know.

PETE: Now, Will—

WILL: Of course, I realize now, I've been foolish. I spent too much on this house, I should have saved more. But I'm still comparatively a young man, you know. Sixty-four ain't old.

CARSON: Who's sixty-four?

PETE: Will.

CARSON: How old are you, Great Uncle Pete?

PETE: None of your business. I don't tell my age.

CARSON: I'm twenty-seven.

PETE: Well, I'm older than you are. I'll tell you that much.

WILL: I gave Bill a hundred thousand dollars at least over the years, and I thought as frugal as he was, he was saving every penny of it, investing it. I don't know what he made on his job. I don't think a whole lot—that is why I gave him money every year, so he would have a nest egg, and he squandered it.

PETE: Now that's water over the dam, Will.

WILL: And Lily Dale giving money behind my back.

PETE: Come on, Will. You're getting all exercised. That's not good for your heart.

[LILY DALE *comes in*.]

LILY DALE: Tom go?

WILL: Yes.

[CLARA *comes in. She has the flowers. She puts them on a table.*]

LILY DALE: Aren't they pretty?

WILL: Take them out of here. I don't want to look at them. Just reminds me of the company.

CLARA: Where shall I put them?

WILL: Take them home with you.

CLARA: Yes, sir.

[*She takes them and goes.*]

WILL: When I went to work for that company, I was twenty-six. And, we just had Bill and I could hardly get by on the salary I made. Somebody told me about the produce company just starting out and needing someone that was a go-getter and aggressive and I figured that was me. I went up to where the business was then and I met Ted Cleveland Senior and we hit it off right away and I went to work the next week and the company prospered. And then he died and his son took over.

[*Pause.*]

You want to know something? His son is no businessman. He's on the golf course more than in his office. You know what I prophesy? I give him six months, a year, now I'm not there and he will lose everything, and that's what sickens me. Forty years of hard work and he will lose everything. Let him get all the twenty-years-olds and thirty-year-olds he wants. They can't prop him up. They can't.

[*Pause.*]

But I was foolish, too, you know. I should have seen this coming. I should have saved money. I don't need luxuries or fine cars and fine houses. I'm a simple man at heart. I'm a country boy at heart and all I want to do is work and now they tell me I can't work. They've taken my work away from me.

PETE: You'll work again.

WILL: Where?

[*Pause.*]

LILY DALE: Will—

WILL: What?

LILY DALE: The money I had left I put in your account.

WILL: Thank you.

PETE: I have a check for you too, Will.

WILL: I don't want your money now, Pete.

PETE: What about your business?

WILL: When I'm feeling better, I'll think about starting a business, and if I do, I'll come to you again at that time.

PETE: Promise me that if you need the money you'll ask me for it.

WILL: I promise.

[CLARA *comes in.*]

CLARA: Miss Lily Dale, that gentleman that was just here says give this to Mr. Will.

LILY DALE: Thank you, Clara.

[CLARA *gives* WILL *the letter, and he opens it. He takes out a check.*]

Is that a check, Will?

WILL: Yes. It's for three months' salary.

[*Pause.*]

I wish I could afford to tear it up, but I can't. It's a hell of a thing, isn't it? You work for a company, give them your life blood for forty years and—

LILY DALE: Not forty years, Will. You went there at twenty-six and you're sixty-four. What's twenty-six from sixty-four, Pete?

CARSON: Thirty-eight.

LILY DALE: Thirty-eight.

[WILL *begins to cry.*]

PETE: Come on, Will. Don't give into your feelings. You're just tired. Now, you're gonna feel differently about all this when you've rested.

[WILL *wipes his eyes.*]

WILL: Thirty-eight years. Where did they go? There was the house on Hawthorne and then the larger house on Kipling. There was—I saw the city growing all around me. There is no stopping it, I thought, and there is no stopping anyone with vision and competitiveness—

[*Pause.*]

CARSON: How big is Houston?

PETE: God knows—too big, I think now sometimes.

CARSON: I met a fellow at the YMCA that said it was going to be the largest city in the South, and I said, "Hold on, mister, I came from Atlanta, and it's going to be the largest city in the South."

WILL: It is like hell. Houston is the largest city in the South, and I tell you what, I give it ten years, fifteen, twenty, it will be the largest city in America, the largest and the richest. If I were only a young man again—

[*Pause.*]

But I'm not a young man. I'm sixty-four years old and I have been fired, and I have to keep reminding myself of that.

LILY DALE: Will, sixty-four isn't old. I'm sixty and I don't feel old at all. I don't—

[WILL *gives her a look. She shuts up.*]

I guess you don't want to hear my opinion.

WILL: I guess I don't.

[WILL *gets up and slowly leaves the room.*]

LILY DALE: Carson, go see he gets back to his room safely.

CARSON: Yes, ma'am.

[CARSON *goes.*]

LILY DALE: My God, Pete. He's still mad at me . . .

[WILL *is heard offstage speaking loudly to* CARSON.]

PETE: He'll get over it, Lily Dale. Give him time.

[CARSON *comes back in.*]

Did he get to his room all right?

CARSON: I don't know. He told me to stop following him around, he wasn't a goddamned baby. Do you really think Houston is going to be the largest city in America?

PETE: I don't know, son.

[WILL *comes back in.*]

WILL: I've got some pride left. I'm not going to take Ted Junior's god-damned check.

[*He hands it toward* LILY DALE.]

Here, Lily Dale, give it to your boyfriend from Atlanta.

[LILY DALE *cries and leaves the room.* WILL *tears the check up. He throws it in the wastebasket as the lights fade.*]

SCENE 4

[*The next day. The lights are brought up on the study.* LILY DALE *is sitting on the sofa with her Bible.* CLARA *enters.*]

CLARA: I met someone who used to work for you a long time ago, Etta Doris Meneffree. A stout lady. Lighter than me. She says you lived in a sweet little house then.

LILY DALE: Yes, over on Hawthorne.

CLARA: She said your son was only a baby then.

LILY DALE: Yes.

CLARA: She said you may not remember her.

LILY DALE: I remember her. She worked for us for almost three years. She must be quite up in years.

CLARA: She is.

LILY DALE: Who does she work for now?

CLARA: She can't work now. Her health broke down.

LILY DALE: Oh. I'm sorry to hear that.

CLARA: She sent her regards to you.

LILY DALE: And give mine to her.

CLARA: She said you used to play such pretty music. She asked if you still played, and I said, "No'm, she don't go near the piano." She read in the paper about your son dying. She said she was sorry. She remembers him, too, as a little boy. She says he was very lively and inquisitive.

LILY DALE: Yes, he was.

[*Pause.*]

Is Mr. Will still in bed?

CLARA: Yes, ma'am.

LILY DALE: Has he had his breakfast?

CLARA: Yes, ma'am. He had it early.

LILY DALE: Did he have it in bed?

CLARA: No, ma'am. He ate in the breakfast room.

LILY DALE: Where is Mr. Pete?

CLARA: In his room.

LILY DALE: Is his nephew with him?

CLARA: Yes, ma'am. Is he going to live here now?

LILY DALE: Who?

CLARA: Mr. Pete's nephew.

LILY DALE: No, he just stayed last night.

[*Pause.*]

What's it like outside?

CLARA: It's nice. Little cool.

[PETE *and* CARSON *come in.*]

PETE: Good morning.

LILY DALE: Good morning.

CARSON: Good morning.

PETE: Will not up?

LILY DALE: Clara says he's been up and gone back to bed. How did you sleep?

PETE: Not too well. Carson kept me up half the night telling me about my people back in Atlanta and what all happened to them. After he went to bed I spent the rest of the night practically thinking over what he told me.

[*Pause.*]

I think I may slip away for a few days, Lily Dale, if it's all right with you and Will, and go back to Atlanta with Carson. I think I want to see it one more time before I die.

LILY DALE: When would you go?

PETE: Today. We'll take the train because I still have my pass. Good morning, Clara.

CLARA: Good morning. How about some breakfast.

PETE: I'm not hungry. I just had a cup of coffee, but I know Carson would like some. Wouldn't you, son?

CARSON: Yes, sir.

[*He goes with* CLARA.]

PETE: Did Will tell you what the doctor said?

LILY DALE: No, Will is not talking to me still.

PETE: He's told Will he doesn't think he can work for six months or so.

LILY DALE: Six months?

PETE: That, of course, is quite a blow to Will. I feel so sorry for him. I offered again to let him have the thirty-five thousand, at least twenty-five of it. I'm loaning Carson's sister five thousand. We talked to her on the phone last night. She needs an operation. I guess her husband don't amount to much. He clerks in a supermarket in Atlanta. Carson is a fine young man, Lily Dale. He reminds me a lot of Bill. He had a high regard for Bill, you know. He said Bill had a wonderful education and was very smart. He said his one regret was that he had never had the opportunity to educate himself. I said it's never too late.

LILY DALE: I thought you didn't believe in education, Pete.

PETE: It's true I didn't use to. Of course, I had to get along without an education. I went to work at fourteen, so I only got to the seventh grade. And I thought I've done all right. I've made a living. I have no regrets. But I think today it's a different world. I think maybe you'd better get an education, if you can. Anyway, I told Carson that I'll help him along if he wants to go back to school. He says he'll pay me back, of course, when he finishes school and gets a job, and I know he will—he's a fine boy. I'd like him to go to school here, but he's got his heart set on the University of Georgia. "Well," I said, "if that's what you want."

[WILL *comes in.*]

Hello, young man.

WILL: Good morning.

PETE: I was telling Lily Dale I'm going away for a few days. Going to leave you two alone if it's all right with you.

WILL: Where are you going?

PETE: Atlanta. Look around and see what's left of my kin. I'll take the train. Like I told Lily Dale, that won't cost me anything but my meals because I still have my pass. Carson says I can get a room cheap at that boardinghouse Bill used to stay in. Carson will stay with his sister. He'll sleep on the couch in the living room as her bedrooms are all filled up with children. Two of them are not quite bright, but he says they have the disposition of saints. He'll watch out for them while his sister goes for her operation.

[*Pause.*]

LILY DALE: Will, do you remember a maid we had while we lived on Hawthorne? Etta Doris Meneffree?
WILL: No.
LILY DALE: A good cook. Bill was five when she worked for us. He loved her so much.
WILL: I don't remember her.
PETE: I don't remember her, either.

[*Pause.*]

We never had a cook the whole time I was married to your mama, even at the last when she got sick. She wouldn't let us hire a cook. She'd force herself out of that bed no matter how bad she was feeling and fix my breakfast. She had to get up at four o'clock, too, because I had to be at work by five. I'd say, "You don't feel well, stay in bed this morning, I can get my own breakfast," but she wouldn't have it. Up she'd get to fix me a big breakfast. The day she died she fixed my breakfast, and when I came home that night I found her dead in the bed. And I went out in the kitchen to call you, Lily Dale, and there was my supper warming in the oven. She must have cooked it just before she died.
WILL: Where is Carson?
PETE: He's having his breakfast.
WILL: Can he drive a car?
PETE: I'm sure he can.
WILL: I wonder if he would mind driving me downtown?
LILY DALE: I don't think you should go downtown just yet, Will. I think—

WILL: I'm going downtown. First Commerce Bank called.

LILY DALE: Will!

WILL: They want to talk to me about a loan. Pete, I am going to ask for that thirty-five thousand dollars now, so I can tell them how much cash I have on hand.

PETE: Will, I'm sorry, but you told me you didn't want that money and part of it I've promised now to Carson's sister. She needs an operation and—

WILL: Oh, yes. I remember now your telling me something about that. I don't half listen these days. How much can I have?

PETE: Well, I promised her five thousand, and I promised Carson I'd loan him some money to get through college.

[*Pause.*]

And I was planning now on this trip to Atlanta.

WILL: Never mind, then.

PETE: I can still let you have twenty-five thousand.

WILL: Never mind. I'll bluff my way through some way. I'll—

PETE: No, I want you to take the twenty-five thousand, Will. I'll feel terrible if you didn't—please, Will.

WILL: All right.

[CARSON *comes in.*]

CARSON: I had a fine breakfast. Clara is a good cook.

WILL: Can you drive, Carson?

CARSON: Yes, sir. I've been driving since I was fourteen. Never been able to afford a car of my own, though. Clara showed me the picture you had made up of Bill. It's a fine likeness. I just thought to myself, life is very strange. Here Bill and I were in the same town, in the same boardinghouse, and we were kin in a way and never ever knew it. My great-uncle was his stepgrandfather. Isn't that something?

WILL: Carson, can you drive me downtown?

CARSON: Yes, sir.

WILL: I'm going to get dressed.

PETE: Need any help?

WILL: No, thank you.

[*He goes.*]

LILY DALE: Do you think I should call Will's doctor and tell him he's going downtown, Pete?

PETE: I don't know, Lily Dale.

LILY DALE: I'll go in the other room and call him. Excuse me.

[*She leaves.*]

CARSON: Have you seen that picture they have of Bill?

PETE: Yes.

CARSON: Do you think it looks like him?

PETE: Well, I believe it was taken some years ago.

CARSON: I didn't want to say anything, but it doesn't look like the Bill I knew. He was very thin and stoop-shouldered, and he was getting bald. Of course he was a great kidder. I used to say, "You're well named because your name is Kidder." I like to go to picture shows, and every night he'd ask me where I was off to. Before I could answer, he'd say, "I know, don't tell me—the picture show." His roommate liked picture shows, too. But Bill never would go. He would just stay in their room and read.

[LILY DALE *comes back in.*]

LILY DALE: The doctor says he shouldn't go. He should stay in his bed and rest for at least two more weeks. Will you tell him that, Pete?

PETE: You tell it to him, Lily Dale.

CARSON: I met Bill's roommate at the YMCA yesterday. He said he'd seen me out here when he came by the other day. He asked how I know you all and I told him I was kin in a way and he said did I know why you all had turned against him and—

[WILL *comes in. He is dressed.*]

WILL: Let's go, Carson.

CARSON: Yes, sir.

[*He and* WILL *start out.*]

LILY DALE: Will. I called your doctor. He said you shouldn't go, not for two weeks. He said you must stay in bed and rest.

WILL: The hell with the doctor. I'm going. Come on, Carson.

CARSON: Yes, sir.

[WILL *and* CARSON *continue on out.*]

PETE: I think he's going to be all right, Lily Dale. It may be the best thing for him. Particularly if it's good news. That will cheer him up and give him something to think about.

[CLARA *comes in.*]

CLARA: Miss Lily Dale, Etta Doris is in the kitchen. She says she would like to say hello to you. Can I bring her in?

LILY DALE: All right.

[CLARA *goes.*]

She's a cook that used to work for us. I told you about her earlier. You didn't remember her.

PETE: Oh, yes.

[CLARA *and* ETTA DORIS *enter.*]

ETTA DORIS: Oh. I don't believe it. She ain't changed at all. Not one pound heavier and look at me. Wore out. Wore out cookin' in other people's kitchens. She ain't changed.

LILY DALE: Oh, I have too changed, Etta Doris.

ETTA DORIS: No, not a day. How long has it been, Miss Lily Dale?

LILY DALE: Oh, heavens. Too long.

ETTA DORIS: An' this your husband. Mr. Will, as I remember.

LILY DALE: No, he's not my husband—he's my stepfather.

ETTA DORIS: Oh, yes. How do you do. You're a fine-lookin' man, so young-lookin' to be her stepfather. Your mama has passed, Clara told me.

LILY DALE: Yes. Ten years ago.

ETTA DORIS: Ten years ago. Mercy. Everything changes. The Lord giveth and he taketh away. And your boy—I was heartsick to hear about it. He drowned.

LILY DALE: Yes.

ETTA DORIS: Mercy. Mercy. We're here today and gone tomorrow. Blessed be the name of the Lord. An' you don't play no more on the piano, Clara tells me.

LILY DALE: No, not since my boy died.

CLARA: She's very religious. She prays all the time.

ETTA DORIS: Bless your heart. Pray for me, honey.

LILY DALE: I will.

ETTA DORIS: And how is your husband?

LILY DALE: He's all right, thank you.

ETTA DORIS: Clara says he had a little spell with his heart.

LILY DALE: Yes.

ETTA DORIS: Well, give my regards to him.

LILY DALE: I will.

ETTA DORIS: I'll be going now. I just took a chance on you being here.

LILY DALE: Thank you for coming by.

ETTA DORIS: Yes, ma'am.

[ETTA DORIS *and* CLARA *leave.*]

LILY DALE: What time will you leave, Pete?

PETE: Four.

LILY DALE: How long will you stay?

PETE: Two or three days. I have a phone number where I can be reached in case you need me.

LILY DALE: All right.

PETE: I'm going to pack.

LILY DALE: All right, Pete. [*Calling*] Clara!

[CLARA *enters.*]

CLARA: Yes, ma'am.

LILY DALE: Is Etta Doris still here?

CLARA: Yes, ma'am. I'm fixing her a sandwich. I hope you don't mind.

LILY DALE: No, I don't mind. How did she get here? Does she have a car?

CLARA: No'm. She took a bus. She still had to walk four blocks. She said she was just determined to get a look at you again.

LILY DALE: Ask her if she's ever heard of Disappointment Clubs here in Houston.

CLARA: Yes, ma'am.

[*She starts out.*]

LILY DALE: And did you ask your friend Lucille if she knew if Mrs. Roosevelt had anything to do with the Disappointment Clubs?
CLARA: I forgot, but I will ask her.

[*She goes.* PETE *enters.*]

PETE: All packed.
LILY DALE: So soon?
PETE: I'm not taking much. I don't have much to take, to tell you the truth.
LILY DALE: I think I'm going downtown for a while, Pete. I have been in the house so much.
PETE: I think that's a good idea.
LILY DALE: If you're gone before I get back, have a wonderful time, and let us hear when you get there.
PETE: I will.

[CLARA *comes in.*]

CLARA: She never heard of the Disappointment Clubs, either.
LILY DALE: Oh. Thank you, Clara.

[CLARA *starts away.*]

Clara, I'm going downtown for a while. When Mr. Will gets back, tell him I'll be here in plenty of time for supper.
CLARA: Yes, ma'am.

[CLARA *goes.*]

LILY DALE: Good-bye, Pete.
PETE: Good-bye.

[PETE *kisses* LILY DALE. *She leaves as the lights fade.*]

SCENE 5

[*Midafternoon.* PETE *is in the den.* CARSON *and* WILL *enter.*]

PETE: Well, I was getting a little worried about you two.
CARSON: I picked up my clothes at the YMCA.
PETE: Well, we still got plenty of time. How did it go, Will?

WILL: Nothing happened. It was just a courtesy call.

PETE: Who did you talk to? Anyone you've known before?

WILL: A boy younger than Carson. I bet he wasn't more than twenty-five.

PETE: Was he polite?

WILL: Oh, yeh. He was polite. But that's about all. He said what he had to tell me, he didn't want to tell me over the phone as he wanted me to understand they had a real interest in me and valued me as a customer and hoped one day to do business with me, but he had to be candid and say this was not, in his opinion, the best time to start a new business, but not to be discouraged and to come back, if I hadn't found another bank interested, in six months and perhaps the climate would have changed by then, and I said, "Do you know you got me out of a sick bed to tell me this?" And he began again about how he felt the telephone was too impersonal and he personally wanted to meet me and make me feel they were interested in me, and then when I left him I ran into Ted Cleveland Junior. He said he'd heard I'd been sick and he was sorry, and I thanked him, and he said, "Did you get my get-well card?" And I said I had, and he said, "We might be able to find something for you with less responsibility down at the company; did Tom tell you that?" And I said he had and I said—

[*Pause.*]

I can't believe what I said.

[*Pause.*]

I said, "I appreciate your thinking of me, and maybe when I'm stronger I'll be around and talk to you about it." And he said, "Well, in the meantime, don't be a stranger," and I said no, I wouldn't be.

[*Pause.*]

Did you eat lunch?

PETE: Not yet.

WILL: Where is Lily Dale?

PETE: She went downtown.

WILL: Are you and Carson hungry?

PETE: I'm hungry. How about you, Carson?

CARSON: I can always eat.
WILL [*calling*]: Clara . . .

[*Pause.*]

What did Lily Dale go to town for?
PETE: She didn't say.
WILL: She probably went over to the YMCA to give money to that boy.
PETE: Now, Will.
WILL: I know. I've been mean as hell to her, and I'm sorry. I just haven't felt well and that tends to make you mean, I guess.

[CLARA *comes in.*]

How about some lunch, Clara.
CLARA: Sure. It's all there waiting. You all ready?
WILL: I'm not eating, you all go on.
PETE: You have to eat, Will.
WILL: I'll eat later. I want to rest now. I can't believe I thanked Ted Cleveland Junior for offering me a lousy job.
PETE: It may not be a lousy job, Will.
WILL: It's one I'll never take. I'll go on relief first.
PETE: Don't say that, Will.
WILL: I'm just ranting and raving. Go eat your lunch.
PETE: Come on, Carson.

[PETE *and* CARSON *go.* WILL *lies down on the sofa. He closes his eyes.* CLARA *comes in, followed by* ETTA DORIS.]

CLARA: Mr. Will, excuse me for disturbing you, but Etta Doris used to work for you all, and she wanted to say hello to you before she goes.

[WILL *gets up from the couch.*]

WILL: Bring her in.
ETTA DORIS: Do you remember me?
WILL: No, I can't say I do. I'm sorry.
ETTA DORIS: I remember you well. You were crazy about baseball. You used to come in every day after work and say, "I'm on my way to baseball practice."
WILL: I sure did. That is right. I certainly did.

ETTA DORIS: You must be prospering, living in a fine house like this.

WILL: We get along.

ETTA DORIS: I hear you been poorly. I'm poorly all the time. It's your heart?

WILL: Yes.

ETTA DORIS: I got all kind of things wrong with me. High blood pressure, arthritis, lower back pains. I can't work at all no more. I'm on the old age. You get your old age yet?

WILL: No, not yet.

ETTA DORIS: I went last week to try to find that house you all lived in when I worked for you. It's gone.

WILL: Yes, it was torn down a while back.

ETTA DORIS: They're tearing down everything in Houston, seems like to me.

WILL: It seems like it. You'll have to excuse me now, I'm feeling tired.

ETTA DORIS: Yes, sir.

WILL: Nice to see you again.

ETTA DORIS: Yes, sir. I was sorry about your boy.

WILL: Thank you.

ETTA DORIS: You were bound and determined to make him a baseball player, too. Did he take to it?

WILL: No, he never did.

ETTA DORIS: Well, I declare. He was a sweet boy. Blond, blue-eyed.

WILL: Yes.

ETTA DORIS: Pretty.

WILL: Yes.

ETTA DORIS: And the friendliest little boy I ever saw. Never knew a stranger.

WILL: Yes, he was very friendly.

ETTA DORIS: Did he keep on that way?

WILL: I think so. More or less.

ETTA DORIS: I went back to see your wife a year or two after I had stopped working for you all and he had just come in from school. She said he was smart. Made good grades.

WILL: Yes, he was.

ETTA DORIS: And I said to him, "You remember me, little boy?" "Yes, ma'am," he said. "I remember you well."

[*She laughs.*]

That's what he said. "I remember you well."

[*Pause.*]

That was a long time ago. I'm sorry I never got to see him again.

[ETTA DORIS *and* CLARA *go.* WILL *is left alone. He goes to the phone. He dials.*]

WILL: Tom, this is Will Kidder. Pretty fair. Look, I hope you didn't tell Ted about our conversation because I've been thinking it over and maybe when I'm stronger I will come in and talk to him. Do you have any idea what he has in mind? . . . Oh, I see. All right. . . . Yeah. I'll see you soon.

[*He hangs up the phone.* CARSON *and* PETE *come in.*]

PETE: We're on our way. I'll call you from Atlanta.
WILL: Fine, Pete.
CARSON: So long, sir.
WILL: Are we going to be seeing you again, Carson?
CARSON: Might be.
WILL: I hope so. Good luck to you.
CARSON: Thank you. Good luck to you.

[WILL *starts out of the room. He pauses.*]

WILL: Carson, would you help me back to my room, son? I feel kind of weak.
PETE: Maybe we shouldn't leave until Lily Dale gets here.
WILL: No, I'll be fine once I get on the bed.
PETE: I still think—
WILL: Go on now. Clara is here if I need anything.

[WILL *and* CARSON *continue out of the room as the lights fade.*]

SCENE 6

[*Later the same day. The lights are brought up on the den.* LILY DALE *is there.* CLARA *comes in.*]

CLARA: Oh, Miss Lily Dale, you're back. I asked my friend Lucille if
Mrs. Roosevelt had anything to do with the Disappointment Clubs,
and she said not that she ever heard of. She said Mrs. Roosevelt was
in Houston once, though. She'd seen her. Got as close to her as I am
to you. She said she was a fine lady.

LILY DALE: I'm sure. How's Will?

CLARA: He's resting. Mr. Pete and his nephew left for Atlanta. They're
thick as thieves.

LILY DALE: Yes, they are.

[*Pause.*]

Clara.

CLARA: Yes, ma'am.

LILY DALE: I've done a terrible thing.

CLARA: What you done?

LILY DALE: I've seen that young man again.

CLARA: Mr. Bill's friend?

LILY DALE: Yes. He was standing in the drive when I pulled out my car
and I had to stop or I would have run over him, and he came to the
car and asked me what had happened to turn me against him, and I
said, "Get in the car." It seemed we drove all over Houston, and I told
him everything that Pete's nephew had told Pete, and he said he was
a liar and he had made the whole thing up because he was jealous of
him, and I said, "Why was he jealous of him?" And he said, "Because
I was Bill's friend and he wasn't." He said, "If I'm so terrible, why
did he try to get me to room with him at the YMCA?" And I said,
"Did you room with him?" And he said, "No, I wouldn't be caught
dead in the same room with him," and I said, "You do have a mother
and a sister," and he said, "Oh yes, a precious mother and a precious
sister," and I said, "What about Bill's praying? Pete's nephew said you
made that up." "And he is a liar," he said. "Ask anybody back in the
boardinghouse who tells lies and who tells the truth." He says Pete's
nephew is known as a notorious liar all over Atlanta.

CLARA: You don't say. Where is that young man now?

LILY DALE: He's hiding out there. In my car. I'm going to try and get
Will to speak to him.

[WILL *comes in still in pajamas and robe.*]

WILL: Where have you been?

LILY DALE: Just downtown. I did a little window shopping.

WILL: You better not buy anything for a while now.

LILY DALE: I know, Will.

WILL: We have a lot of bills.

LILY DALE: I know, Will. How did it go at the bank?

WILL: Not too well. It was just a courtesy thing.

[*Pause.*]

I've lost my spirit, Lily Dale. I know I've been cross with you and I'm sorry. But I have to tell you I am worried. I've just lost my spirit.

LILY DALE: Please, please don't keep saying that, honey.

WILL: For the first time in my life, I don't know where to turn or what to do. Here I am in the finest city in the greatest country in the world and I don't know where to turn. I'm whipped. I'm whipped.

LILY DALE: Will, please.

WILL: I'm not mad at you anymore, Lily Dale.

LILY DALE: I'm glad of that, Daddy.

WILL: But please answer me this one thing.

[*He sees* CLARA.]

Clara, would you mind leaving us alone?

CLARA: No, sir.

[*She goes.*]

WILL: Why did you give that boy money, Lily Dale? Behind my back after I had asked you not to see him again or go near him. Didn't I ask you that?

LILY DALE: Yes, you did.

WILL: Than why, Lily Dale? Why?

LILY DALE: I don't know. I felt sorry for him. He had a sick mother, he lost his job, his sister was deserted with three small children.

WILL: All lies, as we know now. But even if they were true, after I had asked you—

LILY DALE: I know. I know. I have never deceived you before, Daddy, except for one time. It was when you went to Chicago for a business trip and my cousin Mary Cunningham came to stay with me and she talked me into letting two men come over to the house. And you came back from Chicago unexpectedly and they ran out of the back door.

[*Pause.*]

That was twenty years ago. I don't know why I had to tell you that. It has bothered me all these years—not that I would have done anything wrong—

[*Pause.*]

I get lonely, Will. You've always had your work, gone away so much of the time, and then Bill went off to school, and then of course, I had my music, but when Bill died I couldn't go near the piano anymore and I decided I should dedicate myself to God, and then this young friend of Bill's comes and he was sweet to me, and I missed Bill so, and I would always talk to him about Bill. And I never told you this, but just before Alice Temple committed suicide I went to see her and she told me that Bill had committed suicide, that everyone said that, and it upset me so, and I didn't want to tell you because I was afraid it would upset you, so I called his sweet friend in Atlanta and he told me he did not because he had talked to him the night before and all he talked about was God.

WILL: That boy is a liar, Lily Dale.

LILY DALE: He may be, Will, but it did comfort me to hear him say it, and I needed comforting, Will. I've spent my days here crying since Bill died and I wouldn't have done anything in the world to hurt you, Will, because you know how much I love you and how grateful I am for all you've given me, and I do believe in prayer, Will, and I'm going to pray that you get well and strong and you'll find a way to start your business.

WILL: Bill did kill himself, Lily Dale.

LILY DALE: Don't say that, Will.

WILL: I'm sorry, but I think he did.

LILY DALE: You think? But you don't know. What a terrible thing to say about your son.

WILL: Why did he come swimming in the middle of the afternoon in the lake in Florida and walk and continue to walk until he got water over his head? Why? Lily Dale, why?

[*Pause.*]

Lily, Lily Dale, why? I failed him, Lily Dale. Some way I failed him. I tried to be a good father, but I just think now I only wanted him to be like me, I never tried to understand what he was like. I never tried to find out what he would want to do, what he would want to talk about. Life goes so fast, Lily Dale. My God. It goes so fast. It seems like yesterday he was a baby, and I was holding him in my arms, and before I turned around good he was off to school and I thought when he comes back he'll come into the business and I'll be close to him.

[*Pause.*]

I was never close to him, Lily Dale. "How was your day?" "Fine, son, how was yours?" And then he was gone.

[*Pause.*]

I want my son back, Lily Dale. I want him back.

[*Pause.*]

LILY DALE: I know. I know. So do I.

[*Pause.*]

I have to tell you this one last thing, Will. I saw Bill's friend today. He stood in the driveway as I was backing the car out and if I hadn't stopped I would have run over him, and he came to the car and I told him what Carson said and he said Carson was the liar—that—

[WILL *has closed his eyes.*]

He said that Carson was jealous of his friendship with Bill and . . . Will, I haven't told you the whole truth about those two men that came to the house with me and Mary Cunningham. They didn't come to our house because Mary invited them. We were riding down

Main Street in Mary's car and these two men passed us slowly in their car and looked back at us, and Mary said, "They want to flirt, let's flirt back." "Well, Mary," I said, "I'm a married woman, Will wouldn't like that." "What Will doesn't know won't hurt him," she said. "Besides, flirting is harmless." So she stepped on the gas and passed those men and looked back in this bold kind of way, and as she did so, they stepped on the gas and drove right up beside us and introduced themselves, and Mary before I could stop her told them her name and my name, and they told us theirs and they asked us to go to their apartment, and Mary said we weren't that kind of girls, and they said they meant no harm by it, as they just wanted to go someplace where we could talk and get to know each other, and then without asking my permission she said we could all go to my house and gave them the address.

[*Pause.*]

And do you know why I've stopped seeing Mary Cunningham? She said that one time when she was visiting Mama and Pete in Houston, Pete tried to put his arm around her and kiss her when Mama went out of the room. I said, "I do not believe a word of that," and she said the same thing happened to our cousin Mabel Thornton when she was visiting them and their mamas wouldn't allow them to stay at Mama's any longer after that. Do you believe that?

WILL: I don't know. Who knows about anything, Lily Dale? I'm just very tired, that's all I know. Just very tired. Very, very tired.

LILY DALE: Who are we to believe, Daddy? Pete's great-nephew Carson or Bill's friend? Bill's friend asked if you would please see him and let him tell you what he told me. He says he is not a liar, that every word he has said to us is the truth. That Bill was very religious and he did pray loud and clear so that everybody in the boardinghouse could hear him, he said, and he cried as he was telling me.

[*Pause.*]

I feel so sorry for him, Daddy. He's not able to find work and he is alone here in Houston—

[*Pause.*]

WILL: I ran into Ted Junior at the bank, Lily Dale. He said they would like to find something for me to do at the company again, and I wanted to say "Go stuff it," but I didn't. I thanked him, and I have to tell you I may have to swallow my pride and go back there and see what they'll dole out to me.

LILY DALE: Whatever you think best, Will. And you know what I've been thinking, maybe I could start teaching music and that would help us out, too.

WILL: If you like. It might give you something to think about.

[*Pause.*]

LILY DALE: Will?

WILL: Yes?

[*He takes her hand.*]

We're going to make it, Lily Dale. We always have.

LILY DALE: I know.

[*Pause.*]

Will?

WILL: Yes.

LILY DALE: Would you do me one last favor?

WILL: What is it?

LILY DALE: Would you speak to Bill's friend? Let him tell you his side of the story. That is all he asks. Then he says he'll go away and leave us alone forever if you want him to. Would you see him, Will? He's outside in my car.

WILL: No.

LILY DALE: Will.

WILL: No.

LILY DALE: Why, Will? Why can't you just talk to him?

WILL: Because I don't want to, Lily Dale. Because there are things I'd have to ask him and I don't want to know the answer.

LILY DALE: Like what?

WILL: You know the money I gave Bill at Christmas?

LILY DALE: Yes, and that he spent.

WILL: And I told you I didn't know how he spent it. Well, I didn't tell you the truth. In his safety box there were some canceled checks totaling a hundred thousand dollars and they were all made out to his friend.

LILY DALE: Will, maybe there was a reason.

WILL: Maybe so. But I don't want to know what it is. Ever. So tell him that for me. That I know my son gave him a hundred thousand dollars and maybe it was for his sick mother, too, or his sister, but I don't believe it. And I don't believe—anyway, whatever the reasons, I don't want to know. There was a Bill I knew and a Bill you knew and that's the only Bill I care to know about.

LILY DALE: What will I tell him?

WILL: Just tell him to please go away and leave us alone.

LILY DALE: All right, Will.

[*She goes.* WILL *goes to the phone. He dials.*]

WILL: Tom? How about my coming in tomorrow. Early afternoon—all right. I'll be there. Thank you.

[*He hangs up the phone.* LILY DALE *comes in.*]

LILY DALE: I told him, Will. He cried, Will, when I told him. He said Bill insisted on giving him the money, for buying nice things. He said he was like a father to him and he'd never known his father, and that—and he'd go back to Atlanta now and not bother us anymore and he was sorry if he had upset us in any way. He is a sweet boy, Will, I don't care what anybody says.

[*Pause.*]

He said, too, that he wished he could have gone down in the water that day with Bill. That's how much he loved him and missed him.

[*She's crying.*]

Oh, my God, Will, oh, my God.

WILL: Don't cry, Lily Dale. Everything is going to be all right. If I go back to work and you start teaching, everything will be all right.

[*He holds her as the lights fade.*]